The ❧
Half-Blood

A Cultural Symbol in
19th-Century American Fiction

William J. Scheick

THE UNIVERSITY PRESS OF KENTUCKY

Jacket illustration by Charles Bodmer,
from Maximilien von Wied's
Reise in das Innere Nord-America (1843).

LIBRARY OF CONGRESS CATALOGING IN PUBLICATION DATA

Scheick, William J
  The half-blood.
    Includes bibliographical references and index.
    1. American fiction—19th century—History and
criticism.   2. Indians of North America in literature.
I. Title.
PS374.I49S3   813'.009'352   79-4012
ISBN 0-8131-1390-3

Scholarly publisher for the Commonwealth,
serving Berea College, Centre College of Kentucky,
Eastern Kentucky University, The Filson Club,
Georgetown College, Kentucky Historical Society,
Kentucky State University, Morehead State University,
Murray State University, Northern Kentucky University,
Transylvania University, University of Kentucky,
University of Louisville, and Western Kentucky University.

Editorial and Sales Offices: Lexington, Kentucky 40506

For Marion, Jessica, and Nathan

Contents ❧

Preface ❧

Historian James Axtell, in a recent review-essay, remarked the need in colonial American studies for "greater attention to the points of intercultural contact, perhaps through the study of people who travelled back and forth across the cultural frontier, such as 'half-breeds.'"[1] This need exists, in fact, for all phases of the history of the frontier in America. One approach is provided by the literature stimulated by this frontier in the broadest sense or, perhaps, by the *idea* of the frontier during the nineteenth century. Although several important studies of the American Indian in nineteenth-century American literature have appeared, virtually no examination has been made of the half-blood—the half-Indian, half-white who plays a significant role in the popular fiction of this same century. (I have used the term half-blood throughout this study because it is descriptive without conveying any pejorative implication of the sort sometimes associated with the term half-breed.) Fictional treatments of the half-blood are not totally different from those of the literary Indian, but the former do demonstrate idiosyncratic problems and patterns not quite as predictable as one might expect on the basis of the latter. Although related to the Indian, the half-blood possessed certain unique characteristics and provided nineteenth-century American authors with several different literary problems and possibilities. The fictional half-blood, like the fictional Indian, embodied both fact and myth, but in contrast to the Indian, he was not so readily depicted as either a "noble savage"[2] or the barbaric antithesis to civilization. By his very nature the half-blood epitomized the integration (whether successful or unsuccessful) of the red and the white races, provided a dramatic symbol of the benign possibilities or malign probabilities inherent in this encounter.

This book emphasizes the prose of the period because therein can be found the most explicit stereotypes of the half-blood joined to the most artistic experiments with his characterization. In his study of the idea of the Native American, Roy Harvey Pearce concluded that the prose of the nineteenth century was more fruitful than its poetry and drama. The greater flexibility of fiction, I find, proved equally advantageous to literary portraits of the half-blood.

I focus primarily on the *popular* fiction of the nineteenth century partly to avoid the temptation of identifying "the American Mind" with the views of our major authors, but principally because the half-blood emerges as a cultural symbol most provocatively in these works. Although I refer to fiction by such notable writers as Cooper, Poe, Hawthorne, Melville, and Whitman, they are placed within the framework of values provided by the writings of their currently less prestigious contemporaries. For it is in the popular fiction that the half-blood embodies or objectifies, as a cultural symbol, certain general concepts representative of the ideology of nineteenth-century American society. My discussion of the half-blood necessarily involves regional considerations, including differing political, social, and biological notions; but the patterns I identify are designed to be indicative rather than definitive. Indeed, certain perspectives on the collective handling of the image of the half-blood might make specific regional differences a moot issue. This may be the case, for instance, whenever I emphasize the theme of the opposition of wilderness and civilization characteristic of many of the works under discussion, a theme which not only cuts across geographic boundaries but also, and more important, reflects a shared *imaginative* landscape in the fiction of the period. Nevertheless, in several respects regional differences, whether actual or imaginative, seem to exist. Their influence is evident, I believe, in suggestive tendencies or in broad outline, not as fixed patterns, even in the work of southern authors, who more than most seem inclined toward a monolithic portrait of the half-blood.

My study is restricted to the nineteenth century (though I do mention slightly later works by Edward L. Wheeler, Marah Ellis Ryan, and John G. Neihardt, as well as one slightly earlier novel by Susanna Hoswell Rowson) because during this time the half-blood emerged as a very real feature of the American frontier and because authors, many unwittingly but several consciously, wrestled most immediately and vitally with the social and literary problems posed by the half-blood. American writers of the nineteenth century, more than those of any other period, probed into the nature of the half-blood's identity, of his place in the scheme of things (universal and American), and of his future in relation to the New World. Earlier references to him are rare and unaesthetic; more recent portraits—such characters as Dick Boulton in Ernest Hemingway's *In Our Time* (1925), Boon Hogganbeck in William Faulkner's *Go Down, Moses and Other Stories* (1942) and *The Reivers* (1962), Bennie in William Styron's *Lie Down in Darkness* (1951), among many others—may depend to some extent on the patterns established in the nineteenth century, but they relate less directly to immediate cultural issues, have become more abstracted or romanticized, or serve self-conscious authorially-designed artistic functions. In short, later depictions of the half-blood are relevant but are removed from a sense of immediacy to the extent that their inclusion would have dissipated the focus of this study.

I have little to say about the mulatto except in the final chapter, where I compare and contrast the mulatto and the half-blood in terms of their attractiveness to nineteenth-century writers. The list of nineteenth-century works concerned with white-black miscegenation and with the mulatto seems endless; for the 1890s alone one readily thinks of William Dean Howells's *An Imperative Duty*, Samuel Langhorne Clemens's *The Tragedy of Pudd'nhead Wilson*, George Washington Cable's *John March, Southerner*, and Charles W. Chesnutt's *The Wife of His Youth and Other Stories*. The fictional treatment of the mulatto is a concern touching my study at one place or another; nevertheless, his role and the literary strategies associated with it are finally separate and complex matters warranting independent commentary.

The search for relevant works was difficult. There were numerous disappointments, such as Walt Whitman's *Leaves of Grass* (1855–1892), which provided a single unindicative reference to a half-blood in "Song of Myself" (15:282). There were surprises, such as the discovery of a half-blood in Herman Melville's long poem *Clarel* (1876). There were trials, such as reading as many dime and half-dime novels as I could secure and endure; half-bloods appear frequently in these works, usually in minor roles designed to lend local color, exoticness, or alleged authenticity to a story. Although I have read as widely as I could, the risk of any work of this sort is that it doubtless has overlooked some books in which half-bloods

appear. I am confident, however, that the evidence I have accumu-
lated is sufficiently extensive and consistent to serve representatively
for the corpus of works relevant to the subject, and that my conclusions will not be substantially modified by the discovery of some
neglected story or novel. I should also add that I have not cited
every work in which I found comments on half-bloods; many of
the nonfiction tracts on frontier exploration or on frontier settlements and some fictional works were merely redundant when treating the mixed-blood Indian. I tried to select wisely among the writings of the period for quotations, observations, and literary strategies
representative of the half-blood as a cultural symbol.

Every book incurs debts. I gratefully acknowledge my indebted-
ness to my colleagues in the Department of English, University
of Texas, for an invigorating sense of community, but especially to
Joseph J. Moldenhauer, for the painstaking care with which he
read the manuscript, and to Roger D. Abrahams, Alan D. Gribben,
and Daniel M. McKeithan, for suggestions while the work was in
progress. I would also like to thank Irwin C. Lieb, vice president
and dean of graduate studies, for strong support; and the Research
Institute of the University of Texas at Austin for financial assistance
in securing copies of dime novels and in preparing the manuscript
for publication. I am grateful as well to journal editors Robert R.
Kettler, James Nagel, John T. Smith, and William White for the
encouragement provided by the publication of earlier versions of
portions of this study. I also wish to acknowledge the good advice
offered by Kenneth Cherry, James McNutt, and (especially) Bernard
Rosenthal. A special note of thanks goes to my wife, Marion, who
from the first shared my enthusiasm for this project.

1

Twilight Hybrid ❦

Nineteenth-century American attitudes toward the mixed-blood Indian reflect what Edwin Fussell described as a characteristic national ambivalence toward the western frontier in general.[1] More specifically, nineteenth-century discussions of the half-blood reveal unresolved conflicts related to, yet in important respects different from, those centered upon the Indian. Roy Harvey Pearce has cogently demonstrated that the Indian was depicted during this time as morally inferior to the white race and, simultaneously, as ennobled by the simplicity and naturalness of his wilderness existence. Pearce convincingly argues that literary portraits of the Indian provided, finally, only a vehicle for comprehending and justifying the unrelenting sweep of white civilization over the New World. These literary representations amount, in effect, to an evasion of the reality of the Indian, an evasion most evident in the poetry and drama of the period. According to Pearce, nineteenth-century poets and playwrights relied on the strategy "of killing off the noble savage (a matter forced on them by historical fact) and of giving him a vision of the higher and better life which was to come (a matter forced on them by their sense of civilized mission)." The problem for the writer, then, was to avoid making the noble savage envy "inferior" civilized individuals and, at the same time, to depict the rightness of civilization's victory over barbarism. Distancing the Indian from the white race by associating him with the remote past or the far-off frontier provided a typical solution, for it made, according to Pearce, "immediate comparisons and judgments irrelevant and unnecessary."[2] Whereas nineteenth-century playwrights and poets evasively considered the Indian as a part of prehistory, novelists of the period tended to see him as a part of history. Refusing to portray the Indian as either entirely superior or entirely inferior, novelists more successfully dealt with the effects of civilization on the Native American and with the influence of the Indian on the white man. Yet even novelists avoided the reality of the Indian, for in their work the red race essentially embodies an idea, provides a means for putting civilizations into relief, emblemizes what white society has abandoned for better or for worse.

Literary accounts of the half-blood were inevitably influenced by these trends. Unlike the Indian, however, he could not be treated evasively because, whereas the full-blood Indian could be restricted to America's prehistory or history, could be safely confined to the past, the mixed-blood Indian belonged very much to the present and quite possibly to the future of America. The Indian, therefore, might be (in the white American mind) doomed to extinction, but the half-blood represented a new force, perhaps even a new race on the frontier. Since the frontier was, for nineteenth-century white Americans, inextricably (if ambiguously) related to the future of the nation,[3] the half-blood, as a unique manifestation of the frontier, seemed a very immediate reality which could not be ignored. Consequently, prose writers who concerned themselves with him could not bury him in the past, nor could they take easy refuge in the belief that the progress of civilization would displace him as readily as it would the full-blood Indian. Half-bloods appeared to be a new and vigorous (despite biological theories to the contrary) hybrid race which, for better or worse, was evidently a feature of America's future on the frontier.

Not all writers in the century made so clear a distinction between full- and mixed-blood Indians, but a difference nonetheless surfaces in their works. Whereas the *idea* of savagism, a heritage of the preceding centuries' notions of the ignoble and noble Indian, determined a myopic literary treatment of the red race, the *factual* existence of North and South American half-bloods was relatively free from similar long-standing beliefs, other than a sometimes vague, sometimes pronounced contempt for miscegenation. This relative freedom provided writers, and perhaps forced upon some of them, an opportunity to experiment with ideas and devise conclusions of their own. To a large extent, of course, these literary undertakings were influenced by the *idea* of the Indian, sometimes in a totally vitiating way; and then, as well, not every author managed his subject expertly or originally. But, for the student of American culture and art, something rather fascinating did occur; in specific instances something aesthetically vital emerged in a manner quite different from that of works treating only the full-blood Indian. These works posed such central questions as: What is the half-blood? What does he mean? Is he a threat or a benefit to America's promise in the West? The answers varied among writers, often in ways which reflect regional differences. It is not quite accurate to say that all writers saw half-bloods as the embodiment of "the worst traits of both races" and as "the least poetic and the least attractive" of Indian characters.[4] The lowest common denominator of writers' responses, even of the most steadfast assertions about the half-blood, is an ambivalence which kept the central questions about mixed-blood Indians vitally current during nearly the entire century.

Consider Alexander Ross's observations. Ross, who married an Indian woman and raised half-blood children, is, of all the writers I read in the period, the most judicious in his comments on the mixed-blood Indian. Having lived over fifty years on the frontier, he wrote in 1855:

Half-breeds, or as they are more generally styled, brulés, from the peculiar colour of their skin, being of a swarthy hue, as if sunburnt, as they grow up resemble, almost in every respect, the pure Indian. With this difference that they are more designing, more daring, and more dissolute. . . . They are by far the fittest persons for the Indian countries, the best calculated by nature for going among Indians. . . . They are vigorous, brave; and while they possess the shrewdness and sagacity of the whites, they inherit the agility and expertness of the savage.[5]

It was a year later, however, that Ross most fully expressed his opinions of the mixed-blood. In *The Red River Settlement* (1856) he admits that, on the one hand, "they are oftener more useful to themselves than to others, and get through the world the best they can, without much forethought or reflection"; yet, on the other hand, "when not influenced or roused by bad counsel, or urged on to mischief by designing men, the natural disposition of the half-breed is humble, benevolent, kind, and sociable." Later in the book he restates the antipodes of the half-bloods' character:

While enjoying a sort of licentious freedom, they are generous, warm-hearted, and brave, and left to themselves, quiet and orderly. They are, unhappily, as unsteady as the wind in all their habits, fickle in their dispositions, credulous in their faith, and clannish in their affections. In a word, of all people, they are the easiest led astray and made dupes of by designing men.[6]

I have permitted Ross to speak at length in his own words in order to convey an impression of his ambivalence, a trait also characteristic of other writers in the period when discussing the mixed-blood Indian.

This ambivalence may reflect what at least one modern psychocultural anthropologist has described as a pervasive social value in white American society—an unreceptiveness to the assimilation of alien individuals.[7] It is instructive to consider certain selective factors informed, perhaps, by this larger cultural determinative—for instance, the issue of miscegenation. (Usually the half-blood's father is white and his mother is red.) As we shall see, for a variety of reasons (most not very rational) white society in general frowned upon racially mixed marriage or cohabitation; the former was civilly, and the latter morally, dubious to an apparent majority of white settlers. On the whole, such unions were construed as the result of expediency. Typically, W. H. Emory reported in 1857 that the absence of "women of the cleaner colored race" on the frontier eventuates in miscegenation, that "the white makes his alliance with his darker partner for no other purpose than to satisfy a law of nature, or to acquire property."[8] Other writers similarly acknowledge the biological exigency underlying these unions, but generally they tend, especially from mid-century onward, to emphasize the practical motives of "squaw men," who exploited their Indian relatives through political and economic influence in the tribe.[9] Of course, not all marriages between individuals of the two races stemmed from these crude motives,[10] but such a belief nonetheless prevailed among many nineteenth-century Americans and it contributed largely to the outcast status of the mixed-blood in white society. He tended to find himself treated as if his parentage were dubious, as if his hybrid integration of the red and white races betokened bastardy, whether or not his parents were actually married in accord with white or Indian custom.

Ambivalence toward the half-blood also emerged, in part, from the fact that apparently a number of frontier settlements in the early nineteenth century possessed a sizable population of mixed-blood Indians. Timothy Flint, a frontier missionary from Massachusetts, complained in 1826 that the "taste for association between these two races [the French and the Indian] is exemplified . . . in all directions up the Illinois, the Missouri, the Mississippi, and especially Prairie du Chien, up that river, where three quarters of the inhabitants are the mixed descendants of this union." Disturbed as much by the fact of miscegenation as by the intimidating number of half-bloods, Flint derives a modicum of comfort from his belief that whereas the French—for whom he feels a chauvinistic contempt typical of eastern Americans in the early part of the century—demonstrate a natural affinity for the Indians, "there is repulsion between Anglo-Americans and them. Monstrous exceptions sometimes occur, but it is so rare that a permanent connexion is formed between an American and an Indian woman, that even the French themselves regard it as matter of astonishment. The antipathy between the two races seems fixed and unalterable."[11] Presumably the possibility of marriage between a white woman, even of French extraction, and an Indian male is utterly unthinkable to Flint. But the important detail to remark here is Flint's need to explain the presence of a disconcerting number of half-bloods on the frontier, a presence to which Flint and others respond defensively as if they feel themselves to be members of an alien minority.

As Flint's assertion about the affinity between the French and the Indians suggests, the alleged numerical threat of the *métis* was augmented by a tendency on the part of white settlers to associate the white heritage of the mixed-blood Indian with a European or foreign presence in the new world (Anglo-Americans excepted, of course). Time and again, observations on the half-blood convey covert attacks on the French, the French-Canadians (particularly in the Midwest and the Far West) and the Spanish or Mexicans (particularly in the Southwest).[12] This undercurrent suggests that at some level of the white American psyche there existed a vague sense that as long as half-bloods were prominent in frontier settlements, the implementation of American Manifest Destiny would be impeded, for the mixed-blood represented the persistence of both an Indian and an alien European presence in America.

Besides the white settler's semiconscious emphasis on the foreign element of the half-blood's white heritage, his impression of himself as a numerical minority in certain frontier settlements, and his sense of the half-blood as the dubious spawn of unions dubiously established, his anxiety over the mixed-blood was intensified by the fact (noted by Ross) that half-bloods were inclined to be clannish or to ally themselves (or so it seemed) with full-blood Indians. Ironically the pariah status of half-bloods in white society no doubt contributed to this clannishness, which in turn only increased white hostility toward them. Uncertain of their place in the scheme of things, half-bloods frequently suffered from identity problems. As one mixed-blood lamented: "Here am I, neither an Indian nor a white man—just nothing." [13] Even the half-blood's hybrid language alienated him from white settlers. In 1836, Chandler Gilman described this language as "a sort of lingua franca, made up of Indian and English terms grafted on to a stock of most extraordinary French; besides which, it contains some terms which cannot be reduced to either language. Yet withal, it is, perhaps, as poor a dialect as was ever spoken by man, one word often serving a dozen meanings." Clannish bonding permitted the half-blood to express contempt, in a nervous but finally serious way, for both red and white society, in neither of which he felt comfortable. To some extent this verbalized contempt depended on his audience, and it is sadly droll to learn that Gilman was "often very much amused at the tone and manner with which the half-breeds—the vulgar part of them of course I mean—speak of the Indians." Reflecting on how Pelleau and Le Diable, two half-bloods in his party, "never speak of the Indian without some expression of contempt," he concludes, the "pot is ever calling the kettle black." [14]

If the half-blood's problem of identity persisted, however, the ambiguity of his situation gave him at least one major advantage. Because of his dual heritage, which included his ability to speak more than one language, he readily served as a go-between for the two races. This function gave him significant influence over the Indians, who depended upon him to make sense of what the white man was saying and doing, as well as over the settlers, who depended upon him to scout, to secure food, and to negotiate trade relations with the red man. Bernard Sheehan has aptly summarized this situation: "The influence of half bloods rested first on their identification with the tribal interest but also in their capacity to convince the whites that they retained important remnants of civilized loyalty and hence could bridge the gap between the two societies."[15] Such an ambiguous position proved indeed to be a two-edged sword; and both races held the half-blood in suspicion, as if he might at any moment become a double agent. Evidently at times there was good reason for this distrust, though it is impossible to say whether an initial distrust led to abusive practices by half-bloods or *vice versa*. It should be borne in mind as well that although stereotypic imagery frequently reflects real differences between cultures,[16] stigmatized groups tend to capitalize on the power inherent in their marginal status and so strengthen the appearance of conforming to the stereotypic characteristics attributed to them by the dominant group. Three discernible facts clearly emerge: that in general the half-blood found lasting comfort in neither racial group, that his social commitments remained nebulous, and that, understandably, he tended toward his own kind and toward self-advantage.

It has been argued that mixed-bloods found greater acceptance among the Indians than among whites because the Indians' culture generally evinced a social value highly receptive to "transculturites,"[17] a receptivity which intensified white hostility toward them and eventually damaged various tribes. Mary Jemison, a captive white woman who later married a Seneca, explained that she never returned to white society because it would not accept her half-blood children, who were readily integrated in the tribe.[18] During the nineteenth century, in fact, many half-bloods rose to prominent tribal positions, including such men as Peter Pitchlynn and Greenwood Le Flore of the Choctaws, John Ross of the Cherokees, and Alexander McGillivray of the Creeks.[19]

Treaties between the Indians and the United States are instructive in this matter. During the second decade of the nineteenth century, very few half-bloods are mentioned in treaties with the Wyandots (1817), the Miamis (1818), and the Chippewas (1819), and those mentioned are listed individually. During the next decade, however, separate articles pertaining to the mixed-blood appear in such treaties, most notably in those with the Osages (1825), the Kansas (1825), and the Chippewas (1826). This last document departs somewhat from the usual formulaic language by specifically mentioning that "half-breeds, scattered through this extensive country, should be stimulated to exertion and improvement by the possession of permanent property and fixed residences." By the 1830s trouble had apparently developed as a result of the previous policy of granting mixed-bloods rights on the reservation (among other matters, some were reaping financial benefits by violating the integrity of the reservation) so numerous treaties during this decade explicity say that President Andrew Jackson refused mixed-bloods any land rights on the reservation and instead provided monetary allocations for them, sometimes large amounts. This pattern reappeared in the treaties of the following decade, but the problem of the half-blood's political and economic presence on the reservation did not abate. The treaties of the 1850s indicate the failure of Jacksonian policy on mixed-bloods, for they are now again included among those with reservation land rights, with the stipulation that they actually reside in the ceded area (e.g., the treaty with the Chippewas, 1855) or that they have not "chosen to follow the pursuits of civilized life, and to reside among the whites" (e.g., the treaties with the Pawnees, 1857, and the Poncas, 1858). The treaties of the 1850s and the 1860s suggest a governmental effort to transform a dilemma into an asset, for these documents provide for the establishment of such white cultural institutions as churches, schools, and mills.[20] In conjunction with the presence of these institutions, the half-blood was thought (especially by missionaries)[21] to provide a useful link between the white and red cultures on the reservation.

As these later treaties make all too evident, especially in their simultaneous introduction of white cultural institutions and reinstatement of the mixed-bloods, the general receptivity of Indians to the half-blood proved in time to be detrimental to the tribes. Sometimes Indians suffered from deliberate exploitation by certain mixed-blood individuals, but the damage principally emanated from the fact that the half-blood inevitably (even if unwittingly) brought with him various attitudes acquired from the white parent, from association with white society in general, or from formal education in white missionary schools. It is a matter of record that during the middle and late nineteenth century, factional issues within tribes often involved conflicts between full-blooded and mixed-blood members, especially when the issue of tribal removal was under discussion. Among the Choctaws, for example, half-blood Greenwood Le Flore agreed with the Jacksonian decision that his tribe should move and he engaged in a heated argument with the full-blood Mushulatubba over the matter.[22] Even as early as 1826, Timothy Flint witnessed the beginnings of this problem: "In effect, wherever there are half-breeds . . . there is generally a faction, a party; and this race finds it convenient to espouse the interests of civilization and christianity. The full-blooded chiefs and Indians are generally partisans for the customs of the old time, and for the ancient religion."[23]

No doubt benefiting from the fact (as observed in recent anthropological studies[24]) that social distance between groups decreases as spatial proximity between them increases, some half-bloods rose to prominence in white society, as well. Greenwood Le Flore did so, John Rollin Ridge of the Cherokees became a successful writer under the nom-de-plume Yellow Bird, and Antoine Le Claire was one of the founders of the town of Davenport, Iowa, and had the first American locomotive named for him. Early in the century, however, such success was less likely, despite the tendency of the white parent to send his half-blood children to school.[25] Some missionaries may have looked upon the "educated" half-blood as a link between the races that would facilitate the Christianization of the "savage," but clearly even they considered his proper sphere of influence to be among the red, not the white, race. Like their fur-trader predecessors, these missionaries viewed the half-blood solely as a useful agent of the white race rather than as a legitimate member of it. Alexander Ross relates a dramatic instance of how white society expected half-bloods to serve as its agents and of how this very agency generated fears of economic duplicity. The Hudson's Bay Company, according to Ross, forbade members, including its half-blood free agents, to engage in private fur trade with the Indians. The trouble was that half-bloods and Indians also exchanged furs in payment for various services, a common form of barter on the frontier. Understandably the half-bloods considered the regulation detrimental not only to their job of befriending and negotiating with the Indians for the company but also to the normal mode of their private life. Ross agrees with them in this instance, citing the regulation as an example of an exploitative law designed by whites for their own economic advantage at the expense of the half-blood, on whom, we might add, the whites ironically, perhaps nervously and guiltily, depended.[26]

The male half-blood apparently from the first experienced greater difficulty in gaining acceptance in white society than did his female counterpart. Although according to some contemporary accounts, he was likely to be handsome, graceful, and physically well-proportioned, he was considered a pariah by the father of marriageable white daughters; the daughters, if the sketches and tales of the period are any index, were rather attracted toward him. Ross relates a typical episode of a youthful mixed-blood who tried to court the daughter of an official of the Hudson's Bay Company and was reprimanded by the father "for aspiring to the hand of a lady accustomed, as he expressed it, to the first society." The half-blood women, Ross explains, were "invariably fairer than the men, although at all seasons almost equally exposed"; they "are also slender, still more so than the men, but exceedingly well-featured and comely— many even handsome." Ross warns, however, that "at the age of thirty years, they generally look as old as a white woman of forty; perhaps from the circumstances that they marry young, and keep their children long at the breast."[27] Doubtless her youthful attractiveness, heightened by the general unavailability of women on the frontier, made the female half-blood more readily acceptable to male-dominated white society. Other factors influencing her more satisfactory integration into white society include the desire of her white father to see his mixed-blood daughter marry "upwardly" into civilization rather than "downwardly" into squawish slavery and barbarism (he no doubt felt he had socially elevated his Indian spouse rather than lowered himself), as well as the prevailing view of women as passive members of society, a view which reduced white society's sense of the threat of half-blood women. The male half-blood filled a more active, independent, and visible place in the settlements,[28] and more often than not the role he played for white settlers emphasized his Indian skills. To the fathers of white daughters, he often seemed at worst a semibarbarian, at best a member of a class lower than their own. In any event, if female mixed-bloods fared better than their brothers in white society, white male prejudice provided the context for the difference.

Bolstering this prejudice was an emergent biological theory rather similar to nineteenth-century southern arguments in defense of black enslavement. Although many writers of the period agreed with Ross on the handsomeness of the half-blood, few tried to be as fair as he in other matters. The biological argument against the half-blood generally took two forms, one of which emphasized his emotional instability. His "mercurial" nature, in particular,[29] it was believed, often led to the mixed-blood's early death. Elizabeth Fries Ellet, a popular contributor to periodicals and a member of Edgar Allan Poe's circle, tells a typical story of a young half-blood who quarrels over land and who dies (by an accidental drowning, in this instance) while fleeing from his enemies.[30] Life on the frontier was precarious for anyone, but it was particularly dangerous (so accounts would have us believe) for half-bloods, "rather a fickle people, who act according to the impulse of the moment, give free scope to their passions."[31]

Possibly there is some truth to the belief that the half-blood's emotional nature reduced his longevity, but there appears to be no foundation for the assertion that he was genetically short-lived. This second feature of the biological argument against him was frequently expressed in brutally strong language, as, for instance, when W. H. Emory announces that if half-bloods reproduce at all, they engender "a very inferior and syphilitic race."[32] Others were more temperate, or tried to be, and a few (as we shall see) felt an impulse, counter to their prejudice, to discover something new and promising (if not literally, at least symbolically) in the half-blood. Although the biological facts remain uncertain, some biologists and anthropologists have more recently argued that mixed-breeds demonstrate "hybrid vigor," with consequent improvement in physical stature, fertility, and longevity.[33]

It is instructive to turn at this point to Washington Irving's *A Tour on the Prairies* (1835), the product of a journey through Oklahoma in 1832, for an example of how a literary artist of the period recorded his ambivalent reaction to the half-blood.[34] In this work the gradual transformation of an initial distrust of the half-blood Pierre Beatte into qualified, hesitant respect emanates from the fundamental concerns of the book and from Irving's intuitive sense that Beatte represents a hybrid race epitomizing the radical tension between civilization and the wilderness. Throughout *A Tour* Irving contrasts eastern civilization (which he identifies with the white race, light, society, sound, order, permanence, and exterior reality) with western wilderness (which he associates with the Indians, darkness, solitude, silence, anarchy, transience, and interiority), and he localizes this duality in Beatte, in whom both forces are integrated.

A *Tour* is an imperfect work, not only as a result of deficiencies traditionally cited by critics against it but also because it shares with Irving's other works the failure to achieve the sort of self-conscious artistic control we have come to expect in sophisticated forms of literature, even nonfictional forms. Nevertheless, Irving's management of theme and symbol in A *Tour* can be critically scrutinized, especially when illuminated by reference to his subsequent studies of the West, *Astoria* (1836) and *The Adventures of Captain Bonneville* (1837), as well as to his most aesthetically accomplished work, *The Sketch Book* (1819–1820).

Throughout A *Tour* Irving accentuates the asocial implications of the independence and taciturnity of the Indian as well as of the silence and solitude of the landscape by suggesting that anarchy (savage warfare) and transience (nomadic behavior) characterize the western wilderness.[35] Both of these features inform Irving's persistent comparison of his excursion into the frontier to a voyage on an ocean (e.g., pp. 188, 225–26). *The Sketch Book* reveals Irving's sensitivity to the symbolic implication of a journey across the sea; on such a trip, Irving notes, one is "cut loose from the secure anchorage of settled life, and sent adrift upon a doubtful world" where "all is vacancy" and the traveler experiences "the uncertain currents of existence."[36] It is not surprising, then, that Irving's impression of the transience and anarchy of life on the prairies leads him to think of wild bandits, buccaneers, privateers, and pirates (pp. 43, 60, 81), for he is struck by the similarities between the asocial environment of the ocean and "the lawless depths of the wilderness."[37]

More sinister than the "trackless forests" of the New World which he contrasted in *The Sketch Book* to the comforting "footsteps of antiquity,"[38] the "trackless wilds of the Far West" depicted in A *Tour* (p. 5) disturb Irving not only because their deficiency in human presence limits the artist but because they convey a vivid impression of hostility to the forces of civilization. Indeed, rather than a consolation, any human imprint on the prairies arouses caution: "In traversing these perilous wastes, every footprint and dent of hoof becomes a matter of cautious inspection" (p. 108). In this "vast tract of uninhabited country" (which in *Astoria* Irving refers to as "the ruins of a world" [39]) white men can readily grow ill, in contrast to the red men, who thrive in it (pp. 3, 19, 23); the footprints of civilization make no comforting or lasting impression. Whatever the expedition changes, the wilderness reclaims; and so, in one instance, as the troop leaves a site, Irving observes vultures "preparing for a descent upon the camp as soon as it should be abandoned" and he beholds "the wilderness relapsing into silence and solitude" (p. 181).

Particularly disturbing to Irving is the ease with which the wilderness and civilization paradoxically metamorphose into each other in spite of their mutual antagonism. Sometimes the frontier can too readily appear to be a park, or seem "laid out by the hand of taste," or, with a "little stretch of fancy," make buffalo look like "so many cattle grazing on the edge of a common" near "some lonely farmhouse" (pp. 105, 110, 189). On one occasion Irving revealingly confesses "Nothing surprised me more . . . than to witness how soon these poor animals [wild horses], thus taken from the unbounded freedom of the prairie, yielded to the dominion of man" (p. 159). At other times, however, civilization too easily transforms into the savagery of the wilderness, a fact most evident to Irving in the change apparent in easterners who settle in the West. Especially exemplified by the Captain's troop, this change is mentioned in one way or another throughout A Tour but is perhaps best formulated in Astoria, where Irving remarks how "many of these coureurs des bois became so accustomed to the Indian mode of living, and the perfect freedom of the wilderness, that they lost all relish for civilization, and identified themselves with the savages among whom they dwelt." [40] On the frontier white men who do not become ill are inclined to become as beastlike as the Indians, whom civilization treats as "brute animals" (p. 40).

The ease with which the forces of civilization and of the wilderness transpose their identities, as well as the general inability of civilization to make permanent footprints in the frontier frighten Irving, not only because both observations expose, oceanlike, "the uncertain currents of existence" but, more important, because together they suggest that of the two sides of humanity, the interior, anarchistic, and independent self is essentially stronger than the exterior, orderly, and communal veneer of society, that transience rather than permanence defines the true nature of reality. In Irving's disquieting conclusion that "man is naturally an animal of prey; and, however changed by civilization, will readily relapse into his instinct for destruction" (p. 88), the key word is relapse, as it was in the passage noted earlier concerning nature's eradication of any signs of the expedition's presence. Reiterating this inference in *Astoria*, Irving remarks that "having passed their youth in the wilderness, separated almost entirely from civilized men, and in frequent intercourse with the Indians, they *relapse*, with a facility common to human nature, into the habitudes of savage life"; and in *Bonneville* he similarly notes that "the wandering whites who mingle for any length of time with the savages, have invariably a *proneness* to adopt savage habitudes"[41] (my emphasis in both passages).

In spite of the fact that he represents civilization and genuinely fears many of the implications of the wilderness, Irving never escapes a pervasive ambivalence in *A Tour*. On the one hand, he admires "the glorious independence of man in a savage state," the "manliness, simplicity, and self-dependence" of frontier life in contrast to the "luxurious and effeminate" influence of Europe (pp. 28, 53). When comparing wild and domestic horses, for instance, Irving reflects on the "pride and freedom" of the former as opposed to "the poor, mutilated, harnessed, checked, reined-up victim of luxury, caprice, and avarice, in our cities" (p. 116).[42] At times he cannot avoid the suspicion that unlike the frontiersmen, who "in the absence of artificial wants possessed the great secret of personal freedom," "we of society are slaves, not so much to others as to ourselves; our superfluities are the chains that bind us, impeding every movement of our bodies, and thwarting every impulse of our souls" (p. 28). Yet, in the very next sentence Irving cautions that this preceding remark emanated from his "speculations at the time," because, on the other hand, he cannot comfortably affirm anarchistic, instinctive freedom. Even after, or perhaps especially after, personally experiencing the predatory, instinctive destructiveness to which he says all humans are prone, Irving fails to elude the "after-qualms of conscience" (p. 191), for finally he is perturbed by the wild freedom of savage life with its emphasis on the dark inner self, silence, solitude, chaos, and transience. Life on the frontier may have some benefits but only as a preliminary to the refinements of civilization. This sequential arrangement characterizes for Irving humanity's ontogenetic and phylogenetic development; and so Irving ultimately indicates that an adventure on the frontier does not serve as an alternative to European travel but rather should be undertaken by American youth as a preliminary or "previous tour" (p. 53).

Intuitively Irving objectifies this ambivalence in his portrait of Beatte, a half-blood integrating the wilderness (red man) and civilization (white man). "As I had been taught to look upon all half-breeds with distrust, as an uncertain and faithless race," Irving reports, "I would gladly have dispensed with the services of Pierre Beatte," an early view reflected as well by Irving's initial dismissal of Antoine, another half-blood, as a member "of the worthless brood engendered and brought up among the missions" (pp. 16, 17), and by his indifferent treatment of Beatte as a non-central character in the original journals.[43] But in the published version of A Tour, as Wayne Kime has suggested,[44] Irving demonstrates a more balanced assessment of Beatte, eventually speaking of him as "a living monument of the hardships of wild frontier life" (p. 171). He admires Beatte's ability to "shape his own course," to live "perfectly independent of the world, and competent to self-protection and self-maintenance" (p. 20); yet Irving also remarks early as well as late in the book that Beatte "had altogether more of the red than the white man in his composition," that "though his father had been French, and he himself had been brought up in communion with the whites, he evidently was more of an Indian in his tastes, and his heart yearned towards his mother's nation" (pp. 17, 173). Although Irving unconsciously tries to resolve his ambivalence about the conflict between the wilderness and civilization in his portrait of Beatte, his attempt is frustrated, partly because his artistic control in A Tour is imperfect but principally because the asocial implications of frontier life overshadow his admiration.

Although Beatte's divided heritage does not symbolically resolve Irving's sense of the tension between civilization and the wilderness, it does objectify the encounter or nexus of these two forces. For Irving, Beatte exemplifies an advanced representative of the "rabble rout of nondescript beings that keep about the frontiers, between civilized and savage life, as those equivocal birds, the bats, hover about the confines of light and darkness" (p. 14). Beatte symbolizes the twilight existence between society (light) and the wilderness (darkness) led by half-bloods as well as by those half-savage, half-civilized white frontiersmen (figurative half-bloods) who tend to express their divided loyalties by marrying members of the red or even of the black race and thereby fathering literal half-bloods (p. 230). Beatte epitomizes life in what Irving terms a Robin Hood setting (p. 43), an image deriving less from Irving's intention to romanticize the frontier[45] than from his instinctive desire to resolve for himself in some acceptable fashion the conflict he senses between civilization and the wilderness. Like a frontier half-blood, Robin Hood unites the lawlessness of bandits (recall Irving's association of the prairies with outlaws) and the morality of social ethics. This image of the happy combination of the wilderness and civilization underlies Irving's advocation of a "previous tour" of the West for American youth before they travel in Europe. Obliquely and vaguely Irving approaches the conclusion that such double exposure would produce healthy individuals who would form, as it were, an ideal race of half-bloods (in a figurative sense) evincing the best qualities of the frontier and civilization. In this way, as we shall see, Irving anticipates a more sophisticated literary strategy in later treatments of the half-blood.

If he shifted from side to side in A Tour, while unconsciously tending slightly more toward civilization than toward the wilderness, Irving eventually became more certain of his opinion of half-bloods when the memory of his experience with Beatte on the prairies dulled. His attitude toward them darkens in Astoria, where he refers to their "hybrid race on the frontier" as belonging to the "new and mongrel races, like new formations in geology, the amalgamation of the 'debris' and 'abrasions' of former races, civilized and savage" appearing in the "immense wilderness of the far West; which apparently defies cultivation and the habitation of civilized life."[46] By the conclusion of Bonneville, moreover, Irving readily polarizes toward white civilization when he explains that "some new system of things, or rather some new modification will succeed among the roving people of this vast wilderness; but just as opposite, perhaps, to the habitudes of civilization." In fact, he continues, "the amalgamation of various tribes, and of white men of every nation, will in time produce hybrid races like the mountain Tartars of the Caucasus" and "they may, in time, become a scourge to the civilized frontiers . . . as they are at present a terror to the traveller and trader."[47] For Irving half-bloods comprised an ambiguous hybrid race evincing vestiges of the human eveninglike past threateningly haunting America's dawnlike future—a *twilight* race indeed.

Whereas in *A Tour* Irving managed, however, precariously, to suspend his ambivalence in his portrait of Beatte, who as a half-blood living a Robin Hood existence integrates civilization and the wilderness, in *Bonneville* his leaning toward civilization noticeably increases. For Irving five years after his journey, the threat of the western wilderness outweighed the limitations of eastern civilization. Civilization was finally for Irving a necessary, if external or veneerlike, protection from the "uncertain currents of existence" encountered during his excursion into the oceanlike depths of the prairies as well as experienced in his tentative relations with the half-blood Beatte.

Irving, then, reveals an essential reason for his and his contemporaries' ambivalence toward the half-blood: the semiconscious dread that in this mixed-blood, humanity's savage element remains very much alive and might, with a power surpassing civilized restraint, at any moment devastatingly erupt. As Irving's typical associations indicate, the Indian objectified the darker half of the human psyche where irrational undercurrents dominate; at some level of the white American mind in the period, the half-blood emblemized man's divided nature. Herman Melville perceived this factor as the central component in prejudice toward the mixed-blood, and in *The Confidence-Man* (1857) a fictional James Hall explains that in the least harmful Indian may lie the germ of savage treachery: "There is an Indian nature. 'Indian blood is in me,' is the half-breed's threat."[48] One of Melville's ironic points in *The Confidence-Man*, however, is that in a sense everyone is a half-blood insofar as we all evince a bifurcation into civilized surface and savage undertow. The half-blood reminds the New World civilization of what it would prefer to forget, that the savage element residing deep within each "civilized" person as well as within the partially tamed American nation may erupt suddenly and can readily crack the delicate veneer of social order.[49] This fundamental fear is unwittingly evident in writer after writer in the period, but Timothy Flint provides a remarkable instance: "It is a singular fact, that the Indian feature descends much further in these intermixtures, and is much slower to be amalgamated with that of the whites, than that of the negro."[50] Considering the general anathema among whites of the period to miscegenation with blacks, Flint's remark cuts to the marrow of nineteenth-century attitudes toward the half-blood. The half-blood reminded white civilization that the savage element lies latent in all people, that of the two sides of this divided human nature, the dark savage one might readily shatter social restraint. This is what Irving learned on the prairies and described in *Astoria* and *Bonneville*. The half-blood was too actual a presence, too potent a reminder, of the veneerlike fragility of social order, of humanity's capacity to relapse into barbarism.

Nineteenth-century white Americans were, on the whole, hesitant to conclude with the Frenchman Alexis de Tocqueville that "the half-caste forms the *natural* link between civilization and barbarism" (emphasis added), that, like the mulatto, "there is a third race derived from those two, but not precisely one or the other."[51] Ambivalence characterizes their response, with southerners in general expressing more hostility than doubt and with easterners demonstrating a tendency to explore more widely, in factual and fictional accounts, the meaning of the half-blood. Epitomizing this overall reaction is Francis Parkman's anecdotal reference, in *The Oregon Trail* (1849), to mixed-bloods as "a race of rather extraordinary composition, being, according to the common saying, half Indian, half white man, and half devil."[52] To Parkman and his contemporaries, the half-blood was enigmatically more than simply the sum of his two parts.

2

Mother Blonay's Curse ∾

The southern re-action to the half-blood, because on the whole it is so polar-ized, provides a convenient background against which other regional responses can be delineated. In the South, it should be recalled, contact with Indians and trouble over land rights were more extensive than in the North during the early nineteenth century. This fact may have contributed to southern portraits of the mixed-blood Indian as a malignity nonpareil, as a physically and morally grotesque creature antithetical to white civilization. Although some range is achieved, especially by writers in the Southwest, southern accounts tend to conform to Englishman James McKenzie's view of half-bloods as a "most wretched species" in whom combine "all the vices of the whites and Nascapees, without one of their virtuous qualities." Neither Indian nor white, McKenzie continues, they are "like the mule between the horse and the ass, a spurious breed."[1]

Even the half-breed woman, generally treated more benignly than her male counterpart, is not exempt. In "A Dangerous Journey" (1864) John Ross Browne, a world traveller who was raised in Kentucky but who considered southern California his home, tells an exaggerated story of a twenty-six-year-old half-blood woman from Santa Barbara. "Her features were far from comely, being sharp and uneven; her skin was scarred with fire or small-pox; and her form, though not destitute of a certain grace of style, was too lithe, wiry, and acrobatic to convey any idea of voluptuous attraction."[2] But men were mysteriously attracted to her, "worshipped at her shrine," while "women shunned and feared her" (p. 240). A murderer of a rival half-blood woman and (as rumor has it) of her own illegitimate child, she seems a "devil incarnate," a "fiend in human shape" casting a spell similar to "the fascination of a snake" (p. 240). As Browne reflects on her passionate nature, he confesses an inability to determine "which she resembled most—the untamed mustang, the royal gamebird, or the rattlesnake" (p. 241). Browne's story concerns a specific fight between two men over her, resulting in the fatal stabbing of one of the combatants. The narrative ends abruptly with the discovery of the half-blood's body on the burial mound of the deceased combatant, who had been one of her lovers. She has either committed suicide or been killed by wolves, who in any event have "horribly mutilated" her body (p. 246). Hence the half-blood woman, more animal than human in her unrestrained passion, comes to a fitting end.

Dirk Peters, in Edgar Allan Poe's *The Narrative of Arthur Gordon Pym* (1838), similarly exemplifies several typical features of the southern pattern of the half-blood. "One of the most ferocious-looking men" Pym ever encountered, Peters, whose mother belonged to the Upsarokas tribe and whose father was a fur-trader, seems to resemble the *Grampus's* insane black cook, "a perfect demon" in whose league Peters is found during a mutiny. Peters's demeanor is "grotesque"; "the conduct of the hybrid appeared to be instigated by the most arbitrary caprice alone; and, indeed, it was difficult to say if he was at any moment of sound mind."[3] Poe's half-blood symbolizes the irreconcilable antipodes of the human mind: the savage, bestial, insane powers in conflict with the civilized, cultivated, rational powers of the self. The irresolvable antagonism between these two forces in the divided self is a recurrent concern in Poe's work, even as it provides a thematic strand in Pym's confused and inconsistent narrative. Peters emblemizes the fact, as ascertained by Poe, that everyone is, in a sense, a half-blood, that everyone evinces a divided self.

Pym, initially innocent, is initiated into the realization of this fact by his experiences with Peters on the *Grampus*; and quite appropriately Peters suggestively disguises Pym's face with chalk and blood spots. Racial purity, Poe's novel suggests, is in a certain figurative sense an impossibility in the phenomenal world. Indeed, the ending of Pym's narrative, the enigmatic engulfment of its characters by a shrouded human figure with snow-white skin, *may* point to Poe's desire for the South to remain white,[4] but it certainly implies that the tension created by racial bifurcation, in the nation and (symbolically) in the self, will be resolved only by a "destructive transcendence," by an apocalyptic transformation. Like so many of Poe's tales, the vertigo ending of Pym's narrative objectifies an engagement of contesting forces, a dream consummation never in fact realized. In the anticlimactic epilogue of the novel, half-blood Peters (transformed from monster to savior) and chalk-faced, blood-spotted Pym are said to have returned to normal society, where racial cleavage in the nation and duality in the self are related, irremediable, and grotesque features of phenomenal existence.

The ugly reality of racial division in the South is more blatantly present and less artistically managed in Mary Howard's *The Black Gauntlet* (1860), an embarrassingly poor novel defending American slavery as "the school God has established for the conversion of barbarous nations," as "the proudest triumph of humanity and philanthropy in the world's history."[5] Raised in South Carolina and the second wife of the Indian historian Henry R. Schoolcraft, Howard discusses the evil of miscegenation with black slaves as well as red "savages." The Indian, in Howard's view, is more intelligent than the Negro, but his "moral perceptions are as dead as a stone" (p. 495). In this light she emphatically denounces intermarriage between whites and Indians as a "dangerous amalgamation of races," a "suicidal . . . experiment" (pp. 492, 498). While conceding, somewhat atypically for a southerner, that "the half-breed Indian is a fine-looking man physically," she characteristically asserts that "he has none of the redeeming traits of the full-blooded Indian, and none of the virtues of the white man" (p. 540). His brightness and cunning notwithstanding, he proves emotionally unstable, tending towards conceit and drunkenness; "his moral vision never turns inward" (p. 540).

In the novel, Mr. Walsingloss—possibly a surrogate for Schoolcraft, who had previously married a half-blood (Jane Johnston) out of convenience—initially believes that "the union of the American aborigines with the noble Anglo-Saxon would produce the highest specimen of humanity" (p. 541). Eventually, after pondering the recalcitrant ways of his offspring, he realizes that nothing can "make them or Ham equal to Japheth, for God predestinated their inequality forever" (pp. 541–42). Walsingloss's reference to Ham is instructive, for in the introductory remarks to her book Howard expresses a commonplace notion of her day when she speaks of blacks as the descendents of Ham, whose sin of irreverence resulted

in a curse upon his progeny. When she has Walsingloss yoke Indians and Ham's descendents, Howard implicitly denigrates the red
as well as the black race. Indeed, Howard's claim that "a refined
Anglo-Saxon lady would sooner be burnt at the stake, than married
to one of these black descendents of Ham" (p. vii) applies, at
some level, to miscegenation with Indians. Late in the novel she
writes: "The white man sins against the laws of Nature, when he
intermarries with the Indian or the African, for no doubt all hybrids are subject to the same fixed laws of moral deterioration that
the half-breed Indian man almost universally develops" (pp. 540–
41). Half-blood women are spared this fate, according to Howard,
only because they are more restrained by social convention and
"are always short-lived" (p. 541).

   The southern attitude toward the mixed-blood Indian, as illustrated in Poe's narrative and Howard's novel, generally prevails
as well in the fiction of the Old and New Southwest. A short story
entitled "The Scout's Mistake," appearing in James W. Steele's
The Sons of the Border (1872), provides a good example. Set in or
very near New Mexico, the story details the central tragic event
in the life of Mariano, a half-blood introduced by Steele in the
following manner: "As he lifts his head with a kind of growl as
you approach him, you can see that his eyes are sloe-black and
small and wicked, and the whole man bespeaks a capacity for the
doing of deeds as unscrupulous as they are daring"; "as a fair specimen of the admixture of Spaniard and Apache, he offers fair cause
for the hope that the two races have but seldom mingled."[6] Defined by the southern attitude toward half-bloods, Mariano serves
Steele as a character most suited to the wretched fate deterministi-
cally imposed upon him in the story. One day Mariano, who is an
inveterate Indian hater, accidentally shoots his Indian mother,
whom he had not seen for many years and whom his half-blood
lover, Kate (really his sister), was bringing to the village. The guilt
of the subsequently revealed matricide and filial incest reduces Mariano to a gloomy hermit "bankrupt in all the ties of kindred and
love, and striving still in the very luxury of vindictiveness, to
quench the remorse in his heart, and wash out in many an Indian's
life-blood, the stain upon his own red hands" (p. 65).
   Steele's story intimates, however, that Mariano's guilt emanates

from a source deeper than even matricide and incest, that at some level he is vaguely aware of his mother's identity at the time of their fatal encounter; for he had given Kate a crude cross fashioned from memory after one worn by his mother even at the time of her death. This detail, remarkably similar to a southwestern episode in Charles Webber's *Old Hicks, the Guide* (1848),[7] suggests that when Mariano sees his mother, he should, and at some unconscious level does, recognize the identifying cross she is wearing; and we are left with the impression that he murders his mother out of some compulsion. The matricide, in fact, contributes psychological depth to Mariano's Indian hatred; it provides an essential clue to the relation between the unnaturalness of the half-blood's divided self and his compulsion to slay the barbaric or Indian side of himself. Unconsciously Mariano directs his self-hate at his mother, a primary agent in the fact of his "unnatural" mixed blood and of his resultant dubious racial and social status. The matricide manifests Mariano's death wish, and because it originates from the impulse within him to eradicate his barbarian heritage, it ironically only intensifies his sense of fragmented identity and his distance from society. An outcast more than ever before, Mariano does not enjoy even the affection of his sister, who after the death of her mother "had many a lover" (p. 65). The force behind his Indian hatred, ultimately behind his self-hatred, has only been augmented and cannot be directed toward psychological wholeness or social integration.

Steele's portrait is essentially southern: half-bloods are unnatural, physically and emotionally grotesque, the two sides of their heritage hopelessly at war within them. Elsewhere in his book, which alternates sketches and fiction, Steele refers to "the *few* white men who have abandoned civilization and race for Indian society" (emphasis added) and who "have just sufficient humanity left to cause them [like Milton's Satan] to choose rather to reign in hell than serve in heaven" (p. 73). Although he concedes that the Indian occupied the Southwest before white settlers arrived, Steele advances the usual argument that the Indians never tilled the soil and so have no legal claim to the land. The solution to the problem of red–white conflict in the Southwest, he candidly confesses, lies in the demise of the Indian; and this belief touches on the symbolic implications of "The Scout's Mistake." The Indian feature of America's frontier, the story suggests, must pass away completely; coexistence is as utterly unnatural as miscegenation between the two races.

The extent to which the typical southern reaction to the mixed-blood Indian influenced the Old Southwest can be gauged in Samuel Langhorne Clemens's *The Adventures of Tom Sawyer* (1876). In this novel Injun Joe is a half-blood, said to be a "bloody-minded out-cast" who has "sold himself to Satan."[8] A grave robber, liar, and murderer whose principal motivation is revenge, he has set his mind on punishing the Widow Douglas for injuries inflicted upon him by her late husband, who was a justice of the peace. Injun Joe plans to "slit her nostrils" and to "notch her ears like a sow."[9] Avoiding the need for capital punishment while still providing for "poetic justice," Clemens disposes of his half-breed in suitably horrific fashion by having him entombed alive.

Clemens's half-blood, somewhat like Poe's, symbolizes the divided nature of the human self; specifically, Injun Joe objectifies Tom Sawyer's conflicting impulses toward and away from civilization. Partaking of both the savage and the civilized worlds, Tom's fantasies, replete with fiction-fed adventuresome notions about robbery and murder, are as bifurcated as is Injun Joe: half in and half out of white society. Ultimately, Injun Joe dramatizes the self's capacity for savage evil, a capacity romantically imaged in Tom's fantasies and in tension with society. In Injun Joe's demise, Clemens reluctantly depicts the need to assert civilized restraint over the primitive, violent component of the human self. Unlike Poe, Clemens does resolve the tension, however tentatively; but it is interesting to note that the general southern stereotype of the half-blood provides him with a symbol for the ugly side of the human self, the barbaric side sublimated in romantic tales of adventure and held in tentative check by the restraints of white society.

One exception to this frequent southern and southwestern pattern is *Osceola* (1838) by James Burchett Ransom, a resident of Louisiana and later of Texas. To a considerable extent Ransom's portrait of Osceola, who was thought to be (but who was apparently not in fact) a half-blood, was influenced by legends prevalent at the time; indeed, George Catlin, the famous student of Indian culture, spoke of the "heroic Osceola" in terms of these legends.[10] Ransom tends to downplay Osceola's mixed blood and to highlight his romantic, "noble savage" characteristics. Yet, however much he may ignore or minimize Osceola's dual heritage, Ransom does not entirely avoid the issue of miscegenation. The prevalent southern reaction to this matter appears, in an admittedly less virulent form, when Levi Lancaster, a southern youth who is a surrogate for the narrator of the novel, falls in love with an Indian, "the fair Ouskaloosa."[11] Strikingly beautiful in person and manner, Ouskaloosa's "artless innocence, and the intelligence and sweetness of her sprightly countenance, revealed a delicacy of feeling, a dignity of spirit, and nobleness of soul, which but few could acquire in the highest and most exalted walks of civilized society" (p. 18). Lancaster would marry her "were it not for the opinions of the mean, selfish world." Being a proper southern gentleman, he lets her go, and she later becomes the meet wife of Osceola. The issue of miscegenation surfaces again in the novel when Cuptchohula, an Uchee chief, speaks contemptuously of intermarriage between the red and white races, asserting that the mingling of the two bloods guarantees fatal consequences. Most significantly, when Osceola learns of his mixed blood, he is overcome "with consternation and astonishment, equal to terror" (p. 67).

Ransom's may be, for whatever reasons, the most temperate of the southern and southwestern fictional treatments of the half-blood. The antimiscegenation sentiment in the book remains, but the narrator's emphasis on the waste of Osceola's inherent nobility transcends regional definition and might serve as a refrain for the fiction of countless nineteenth-century American writers who depicted the "noble savage" in some fashion:

What a pity . . . that a youth of such sprightliness and promise should be deprived of the inestimable benefits of education, so necessary to mature those bright germes of genius, that are destined to spring forth and luxuriate beneath the obscuring clouds of ignorance and superstition; and that he should be excluded from the advantages of civilization and enlightened society, which would not only soften and moralize the heart, but would bring into requisition all of those ennobling qualities and virtuous passions that belong to human nature, which alone can properly elevate and dignify man. [pp. 53–54]

The loss is to be rationally bemoaned, but it is, in southern and in southwestern works, often outweighed by emotional hostility to miscegenation. And so, finally, Ransom's confinement of his half-blood to an Indian context may reflect legend or history, may even convey a message about the waste of "bright germes of genius," but it also exemplifies a strategy of evasion. The narrator, whose fictional surrogate pulls back from a miscegenous relationship with Ouskaloosa, resolves Osceola's terror-filled realization of his mixed blood by ignoring it finally and by presenting his protagonist as if he were a full-blooded Indian. Because it is influenced by legends Ransom cannot modify, this evasion may be the mildest version of the pattern we have remarked, a pattern usually requiring the physically and morally grotesque half-blood to die (or at best to survive, like Mariano, in a living death) because of biological deficiencies or as a result of the proper manifestation of white social justice. Ransom's pattern may be more temperate, but it is still southern in temperament.

The strategy of evasion is also evident in *The Rangers and Regulators of the Tanaha* (1856) by Alfred W. Arrington, who spent most of his life in North Carolina, Arkansas, Missouri, and Texas. Set in Texas, near Louisiana, the novel recounts the adventures of William Bolling from Alabama, who is "a great, great granson, or sumthin of the sort, of old Pocahontas." [12] Bolling is not a half-blood, but Arrington gives him a trace of specifically American exoticness and modifies the general southern fictive pattern in treating mixed-blood Indians by relating him to the legendary Pocahontas, who even very early in the century, in Joseph Croswell's A New World Planted (1802), had been said to be "browner than European dames,/ But whiter far, than other natives are." [13] Even today many prominent Virginia families trace their ancestry to the son of Pocahontas and her white husband, John Rolfe. In the American imagination, Pocahontas, as even Croswell's remark indicates, had been so transformed into a romantic figure that the reality of her Indian nature could be effectively ignored. Arrington benefits from this evasion in his portrait of Bolling, and his attitude toward the red race (and presumably toward half-bloods) emerges in his portrait of Comanche Ben, a lawless Indian of "supreme ugliness" who was captured as a boy and raised among whites but who "retained the complexion, the instincts, and many of the habits characteristic of his savage origin":

His broad, low, massive frame, although denoting great strength, and really possessing much activity, was horribly misshapen with crooked bones and angles, depriving it of all comparison with any specimen of the animal kingdom, unless it might be likened to that of a lean wolf standing on its hind legs. His face was still worse, revealing the bony contour of the Indian physiognomy, increased, however, to an extreme that looked absolutely hideous. . . . his snake-like leering eyes crossed each other almost at right angles. [pp. 125–26]

Bolling is exempt from association with such innate corruption. At the end of the novel someone remarks that Bolling does not "take arter the old injun grandmother," that within him is "the grit of the white great grandaddy" (p. 396). He possesses only the merest trace of Indian blood, generationally diluted, and that trace safely comes from Pocahontas, who seemed more white than red to the American imagination, even in the South.

A similar evasive maneuver occurs in *The Phantom Mazeppa* (1882), a novel by Prentiss Ingraham (under the pseudonym Dangerfield Burr). The work focuses on Sancho, a half-blood whose real name is Gila Alcolo and whose nature is decidedly ambiguous. Sancho's body is "as sinewy as a panther's, and his motions as noiseless as a snake's, while his darkly bronzed face and piercing eyes proved him to possess a courage that was undaunted, and a heart that was merciless toward a foe." [14] Later in the novel, the half-blood's mixed traits are emphasized: "As one studied the face of Sancho, it would improve in character and looks, for there was that in it which gave the idea of strength, resolution, and yet not devoid of art, though it was stamped with recklessness, dissipation, and a certain sadness" (p. 19).

Ingraham wants to make Sancho a heroic figure, especially when the half-blood seeks vengeance for the alleged seduction of his sister by Carter Conrad. But even in 1882, Ingraham, who spent his life in Mississippi and Maryland, feels the tug of the apparently prevalent southern attitude toward the mixed-blood Indian, and his solution for this tension between cultural convention and artistic design lies in a sleight of hand: the silent, probably unconscious, transformation of Sancho's Comanche mother (p. 3) into an Aztec Indian. As a descendent of the legendary aristocratic Aztecs, Sancho possesses an inherent nobility (however qualified in fact by Aztec practices), and indeed in the last half of the novel Sancho becomes a complete romantic hero.[15] Ingraham eases the tension further by having Sancho leave Nebraska for the land of his Mexican father. In Mexico, rather than in America, he will fully manifest the nobility of his Aztec heritage. Ingraham covertly suggests that Mexico, "that tumultuous, even fickle land" (p. 23), is the proper place for a half-blood combining an unstable mixture of Aztec nobility and barbarism; indeed, many nineteenth-century Americans believed Mexicans to be biologically Indian.[16] By transforming the Comanche present of Sancho's heritage into a legendary Aztec past and by removing his white heritage from America to Mexico, Ingraham manages to obviate the problems usually inherent in the depiction of his exotic protagonist.

"Loka" (1892), a short story included in Kate Chopin's *Bayou Folk* (1894), also illustrates how the southern pattern is sometimes mutated in southwestern fiction of the nineteenth century. This story concerns a homeless, apathetic half-blood teenager, whose "coarse, black, unkempt hair framed a broad, swarthy face without a redeeming feature, except eyes that were not bad."[17] Loka works as a lowly servant on a farm, is despised by her mistress, and dreams of escaping into the wild woods. Momentarily entranced one day, she nearly does run off, but fondness for the mistress's baby prevents her, somehow even obviates her nearly instinctive attempt to kidnap the child. In her unpleasant physiognomy as well as in her big-boned, clumsy body, Loka is a physical misfit even as she is a social pariah; and in these matters she readily partakes of the general southern pattern of half-blood portraits.

Chopin, however, tends to be more interested in psychology and character than in social issues per se,[18] and "Loka" is more concerned with the essential humanity of its protagonist than with any point about miscegenation or racial prejudice. Loka may indeed be "*une pareille sauvage*," as her mistress calls her (1: 216), but she also possesses inherently redemptive human features, as evinced in her consuming affection for the baby which determines finally her renunciation of primitive forest freedom for civilized social bondage. The master of the farm perceives this redemptive feature and gently instructs his wife to treat Loka more kindly, so that the emergent humane, civilized element in her may eventually supplant her "Injun" self. "We got to rememba she ent like you an' me, po' thing;

she's one Injun, her" (1:218). Chopin's portrait is benign in its emphasis on Loka's essential humanity—and this is an important distinction—but its background or context utilizes the southern pattern in fictive treatments of half-bloods.

The prevalent southern fictional characterization of the half-blood is typified in William Gilmore Simms's *The Partisan* (1835) and *Mellichampe* (1836), in which Ned Blonay is portrayed as an epitome of evil. For Simms, the half-blood and the mulatto are equivalent threats to the purity of white civilization in America. In both of these novels, set in South Carolina, the theme of America's preservation of political purity during the Revolutionary War is coalesced with the subtheme of the white South's need to maintain racial purity.

Goggle, as Ned Blonay is called in the romances, might be described as a peripheral character; but because he functions as a nexus for several motifs emanating from the works' themes, he cannot be dismissed as merely a manifestation of local color or of Gothic tradition.[19] Simms depicts Goggle without an iota of sympathy, emphasizing the "strange protrusion of his eyes [giving] his face a gross and base expression" and eliciting "distrust, or even dislike, in the mind of the observer."[20] Simms continues: "Goggle was as warped in morals as he was blear in vision; a wretch aptly fitted for the horse-thief, the tory, and murderer. His objects were evil generally, and he had no scruples as to the means by which to secure them" (p. 178). Simms's allusion to Tories should not be overlooked because throughout both novels the British invaders and their American allies are associated with Goggle's moral deficiences.

Chief among Goggle's vices is a consuming desire for revenge, rather similar to that of Injun Joe in *The Adventures of Tom Sawyer* and, more obliquely, of Mariano in "The Scout's Mistake" (both published much later in the century). As William Humphries, a hero in Simm's two books, observes about Goggle: "The worst is, he fights with a bad heart, and loves to remember injuries. I do believe they keep him from sleep at night. He's not like our people in that; he can't knock away at once, and have done with it, but he goes to bed to think about it, and to plan when to knock, so as never to have done with it. He loves to keep his wrongs alive, so that he may always be revenging" (p. 97). The revenge motif is an important component of the themes in the two novels, and it is significant that Humphries, who in *Mellichampe* relents in seeking cruel and fatal revenge on Goggle, particularly distinguishes "our people"—the Americans fighting for independence—from Goggle in this matter. In *The Partisan* Major Robert Singleton, a leader of the colonial troops who takes to heart his sister Emily's dying words about mercy, emphasizes the need for Christian forbearance when it comes to retaliation. Time and again he echoes Emily's sentiments, most notably when he admonishes his troops just prior to their attack on the British (pp. 165, 272, 373). Simms contrasts this "American" attitude with the revengeful atrocities of the British, which deeds we are meant to associate with Goggle's bestial behavior and with that of Frampton, the "splendid savage" (p. 78) who went insane as a consequence of the fatal British brutality inflicted upon his wife and who now seeks maniacal revenge on his enemies.

At the heart of Goggle's viciousness is, as Humphries remarks, his bad blood—not his lack of heritage[21] but his dual heritage. Rumor has it, according to Humphries, that Goggle's father was either a mulatto or an Indian (p. 97). In fact he was a Catawba Indian, but the failure of the novel's southern character to differentiate between Goggle's Indian or Negro descent is telling; for in Simms's view no distinction needs to be made.[22] Early in *The Partisan* Simms explicitly yokes the two races in terms of their alleged mutual inhumane characteristics: "Negroes and Indians formed allies, contributing, by their lighter sense of humanity, additional forms of terror to the sanguinary warfare pursued at that period" (p. 53). As this observation also suggests and as the entire novel makes abundantly clear, Simms associates this black and red brutality (especially in the matter of revenge) with British warfare, particularly as waged by Captain Huck, who oversees "the cold-blooded execution of hundreds" (p. 54), and by Tarleton, who orders the slaughter of surrendering rebels (p. 373). When Major Singleton rallies his forces, he refers to the British as "brutes," passionately arguing: "I do not call upon you to destroy men, but monsters; not countrymen, but those who have no country—who have only known their country to rend her bowels and prey upon her vitals" (pp. 372–73). The British and their allies (their occasional human features notwithstanding) are finally as morally warped as is Goggle, "the beast" (p. 176), "the indifferent savage" (p. 206); and all of them are as insane as the maniacal "savage" Frampton.[23]

Goggle, then, serves as a nexus for Simms's related themes of the threat to American political purity posed by British occupation and the threat to the purity of southern white civilization posed by the possibility of racial miscegenation. These related themes most dramatically intersect in the episode concerning Mother Blonay's curse. Goggle's mother, who is believed to be a witch and who is said to belong to a social class "little above" the slaves (p. 224), places a curse upon Humphries's sister, Bella, in retaliation for an insult against her son. The curse is oblique and elliptical: "Goggle—Goggle—Goggle—*that* of her!" (p. 189). Following the curse, Humphries is plagued with fears about his sister's honor; but the significance of the curse and of his fears becomes evident later, when Mother Blonay lures Bella into the forest and abandons her to Hastings, a British sergeant who attempts to rape her (p. 232). Hastings's brutality and moral depravity again recall Simms's intentional association of British with barbaric red and black behavior, a connection underscored by Mother Blonay's parting words to betrayed Bella: "Cry away—Goggle now—Goggle now—Goggle now —scream on you poor fool" (p. 232). Hastings's attempted rape of the sister of one of the novel's American heroes objectifies in small the larger effort of the British to brutalize the American land, which is portrayed as if it were feminine.[24] And Mother Blonay's curse, with its elliptical references to her half-blood son, obliquely condemns the South, as represented by Bella, to the grotesque (Goggle-like) result of miscegenation—of political miscegenation with the British and of racial miscegenation with a soldier whose British identity has been associated by Simms with Indians and Negroes.

Had Mother Blonay and Hastings been successful, Bella (a true southern belle) not only would have been deflowered but might even have given birth to, so to speak, a mixed-blood child, whose British side would be figuratively equivalent to the Indian or (as some would have it) the black side of Goggle. This is the ultimate threat behind Mother Blonay's curse. But, the novel tells us, southern America is not to be a region of half-bloods any more than the nation as a whole is to be a place of political "half-breeds"; Simms has Bella rescued by her brother and then safely married to John Davis, a loyal American revolutionary. For his southern audience, already greatly enflamed in the 1830s by arguments about slavery, Simms's message was that, just as America's political purity had been preserved by the preceding generation, so too must the white South be rescued from the current threat of interracial pollution.

A rescue as symbolically significant as Bella's occurs in Simms's "The Two Camps," which was printed in *The Wigwam and the Cabin* (1845). This story tells of the affection of an Indian named Lenatewa for the white daughter of Daniel Nelson. Nelson admires the young Indian, remarking in particular his "natural sort of grace and dignity" so rare in a white man. But earlier in his life Nelson had experienced a disturbing vision in which he saw a white woman, with a face "bright like any star," sitting in the center of an Indian camp. "I never was in such a fix of fear and weakness in my life," he recalls, "I felt sure that this sign hadn't been shown to me for nothing." [25] Eleven years later he actually sees his daughter Lucy (whose name recalls the star image in his vision) held captive in an Indian camp. Lucy's literal captivity, however, does not unveil the entire meaning of Nelson's vision. Its essential message becomes evident when his wife, in contrast to her husband, vehemently opposes Lucy's marriage to Lenatewa. Simms resolves this situation by having the two lovers ambushed. Lenatewa dies from a wound, and Lucy, who never marries anyone, is saved from the horror of miscegenation. Simms's readers, like Nelson, have been shown this "vision" for a reason. An explication of its message, one can suggest, is provided by Hugh Grayson in *The Yemassee* (1835): "It is utterly impossible that the whites and Indians should ever live together and agree. The nature of things is against it, and the very difference between the two, that of colour, perceptible to our most ready sentinel, the sight, must always constitute them an inferior caste in our minds." [26]

Simms believed that fiction proves valuable "when it ministers to morals, to mankind, and to society." [27] In *The Partisan* and *Mellichampe* the half-blood serves as a touchstone for Grayson's homily. Goggle provides a focal point not only for the revenge–mercy motif prevalent in the two novels but also for the Indian–Negro–British motif contributing to Simms's broad allegory about the threat of miscegenation to the American culture (mixing British and American ways) and to the southern white race (mixing black or red with white blood). Compared with Poe's symbolically suggestive but inadequately developed Dirk Peters, with Howard's unregenerate two-dimensional mixed-bloods, with Steele's compulsive Mariano, with Clemens's stereotypic Injun Joe, with Chopin's *pareille sauvage*, and with Ransom's, Arrington's and Ingraham's evasively drawn protagonists, Simms's Goggle emerges as the quintessential and most aesthetically managed prototype of the cursed, grotesquely unnatural half-blood of nineteenth-century southern fiction.

3

Symbolic American Prototype ✒

A few writers from the northeastern and middle-eastern United States expressed views similar to the southern and southwestern reaction to the mixed-blood Indian. Timothy Flint, who peripherally registers his disapproval of miscegenation in a novel entitled *Francis Berrian* (1826), epitomizes this group when, as we saw in the first chapter, he deplores in his *Recollections* the "unnatural" interbreeding between the two races and, at the same time, defames the French in particular for their alleged affinity for Indian mates. Flint, it should be remembered, had asserted that Indian features integrate with white characteristics less well than do those of the black race. Even Alexander Ross, an easterner who spent most of his life in the Old Northwest and who (his ambivalence notwithstanding) discusses half-bloods more comprehensively than any of his contemporaries, confessed during an atypical moment that "they form a composition of all the bad qualities of both" races.[1]

Robert Montgomery Bird, a resident of Philadelphia, might also be placed in this group. *A Belated Revenge*, begun by Bird in 1837 but later edited by his son in 1889, presents a minor character, most often called Jack, who is a half-blood akin to his southern confreres. A grotesque "imp" who murders the narrator's brother and delights in tormenting animals, Jack possesses "a most wicked, mischievous, malicious countenance," according to Ipsico Poe—"the most terrible head and face I had ever seen."[2] Because Bird left the manuscript of this story unfinished, several details in the work remain uncertain, including whether Jack is in fact the son of Craven Poe, Ipsico's infamous renegade relative who nearly succeeds in destroying all of Ipsico's family and friends. Also unclear is whether Craven is a mixed-blood Indian. He is said to be an "Indian-souled scoundrel" and, twice in the work, he is briefly referred to as half-Indian; but the context for these remarks suggests that they do not refer to literal fact but are used figuratively as a form of disparagement.[3] In any event, Jack, definitely a mixed-blood, and Craven, Jack's probable father, who is said to have a villainous Indian nature, portray the half-blood of southern tradition. If they are not father and son in fact, they are related through family-like association and in diabolical spirit. As paragons of evil, they provide the means whereby Ipsico's innocent eyes (in later years he admits he could never see even what was under his nose) are opened to the darker features of the human self and of reality.[4] Through them Ipsico is initially estranged from his family and from himself. In fact, Craven, who tells Ipsico that he intends to be a father to him, replaces the youth's real father, from whom Ipsico withdraws; and this new familial identity initiates him, through violence and death (including Ipsico's figurative demise), into self-awareness and reality.[5] At the end of the tale Ipsico slays Craven and Jack, makes spiritual peace with his deceased father, and adopts Nelson, a frontiersman of heroic proportions, as a surrogate father. With his eyes opened to the dark side of himself and of the world, Ipsico will now follow Nelson into the wilderness. In short, Ipsico eradicates his ties with the perverse half-human, half-savage family of Craven and Jack for identity with the socially and morally defined company of his last surviving brother and of Nelson.

Bird's racial views are difficult to codify, and so whether his use of the half-blood (literally in Jack, figuratively in Craven) was also designed to convey a message about racial pollution must remain moot. On the one hand, he could write an antislavery play (The Gladiator, 1831); on the other hand, he feared the brutality of blacks struggling for freedom and resolved to leave Pennsylvania if they were given the franchise there.[6] He had travelled extensively, with aroused feeling, through the South and the Old Southwest; and his fiction readily reveals the frontier views he encountered in these regions. A Belated Revenge, it should be noted, is set in Virginia, and its narrator claims to have written the work in Kentucky. Moreover, not only did Bird read The Yemassee and correspond with its author, but he reflects typical frontier hostility toward Indians, most notably in Nick of the Woods (written in 1837, the same year he started A Belated Revenge), in which they are referred to as "red niggurs." In A Belated Revenge there is, to my mind, no apparent admonition against miscegenation, as there is in Simms's work; nonetheless, for symbolic and possibly other reasons, Bird's short novel relies on the general southern caricature of the half-blood.

Perhaps the most surprising of those easterners who depict the half-blood in this fashion is Walt Whitman. Looked at from one perspective Whitman's "The Half-Breed" (1846), originally entitled "Arrow-Tip" (1845),[7] was doubtless designed to dramatize the horror of capital punishment.[8] Its original title signals the reader to focus on Arrow-Tip, the Indian who dies as a result of mistaken testimony, revenge, and a precipitate legal hanging. But another dimension exists in the story, a less obvious theme which Whitman emphasized when he republished the story about a year later under a new title.[9] The revised title in no way negates the attack on capital punishment in the story, but it does remove Arrow-Tip from the announced center of attention. The new title suggests that the central protagonist is Boddo, the passionate, revengeful hunchback half-blood; and the theme informing his portrait from the first is now highlighted by Whitman, who in 1846 was devoting more of his attention to the problem of slavery and its racial implications. This theme concerns the grotesque unnaturalness of racial amalgamation.[10]

At best, Whitman was ambivalent about the American Indian. To him, as Leadie Clark has remarked, "That the Indian was disappearing was regrettable but right, for it was a circumstance that could not be prevented."[11] "The Half-Breed," which Clark does not mention, reveals Whitman's sympathy for the plight of the vanishing Indian, most particularly in the only genuinely touching scene in the work, the conversation between Arrow-Tip and his brother, the Deer. The Deer laments, "O, brother, the Great Spirit has frowned upon our race. We melt away, like the snows in spring," to which Arrow-Tip resignedly replies, "It is the will of the Spirit."[12] In a brief epilogue to the story we are told (presumably of the Deer) that "an Indian leader, the remnant of his family, led his tribe still farther into the west, to grounds where they never would be annoyed, in their generation at least, by the presence of the white intruders" (p. 291). Clearly Whitman sympathizes with the dispossessed Indians, but his sense of their doom as "the will of the Spirit" is equally evident; moreover, the qualification, "in their generation at least," not only stresses the inevitability of the conflict between the white and red races but also forecasts that the outcome will recapitulate Arrow-Tip's death at the hands of white civilization.

Whitman sees no other resolution. Just as he would explicitly assert in 1858 that "nature has set an impassable seal against" the amalgamation of whites and blacks in America,[13] so too in this early story Whitman implies that racial separation is an unalterable natural law governing relations between the white and red civilizations. The grotesque result of unnatural interbreeding of the races is an underlying theme of "The Half-Breed."

Boddo, who is the son of Father Luke and an Indian associated with Arrow-Tip's tribe (pp. 265, 272), actualizes this theme. Everyone who sees him experiences "some doubt whether to class this strange and hideous creature with the race of Red Men or White" (p. 258), but no one hesitates to denounce him, not even Father Luke. Boddo, whose deformed physical features and warped morality objectify Whitman's view of the half-blood's unnaturalness, belongs neither to nature (hence his deformities) nor to civilization (hence his warped morality). Rather than a participant in both races, he is a pariah among the settlers and the Indians alike, a fact made most manifest at the end of the story: "Scorned and abhorred by man, woman, and child, the half-breed, through whose malicious disposition the fatal termination took place . . . , fled the settlement of Warren. Whether he perished in the wilds, or even now lives a degraded and grovelling life, in some other town, no one can tell" (p. 291).[14] But this passage does tell us, once again, that the half-blood is not at home in the wilds of nature or in the towns of civilization. Boddo is indeed a "monstrous abortion" (p. 272), unnatural in every regard; and not only is he an outcast from the two races joined in him, but he in fact appropriately serves in the story as the immediate instrument of the friction between the races. His actions intensify the conflict between the Indians and the settlers, resulting in the symbolic death of Arrow-Tip (foreshadowed by the death of Boddo's mother while giving birth to him) and in the equally symbolic removal of Arrow-Tip's tribe. The Indians must decline and die because they are different from the stronger white race, because racial friction is reality, and because racial amalgamation (Boddo) is an unnatural "monstrous abortion."

So far as we know, Whitman never met any half-bloods from

the frontier,[15] so his portrait of Boddo remains something of a curiosity. No doubt the southern angle of vision in the story is related to what Whitman once spoke of as "the New York feeling with regard to anti-slavery." Jerome Loving has aptly designated this as anti-black sentiment which, during the poet's Brooklyn years, tainted his attitude toward the American Negro.[16] Indeed, Whitman's characterization of Boddo evinces an affinity with contemporary southern portraits of the half-blood, especially with Simms's depiction of Goggle in The Partisan and Mellichampe. In physical and moral deformity, in the matter of revenge, and in the unmitigated grotesqueness of his portrait, Boddo is remarkably similar to Simms's half-blood. Although Whitman's conscious imitation of others in his early stories is well known, at present no sound case can be made for Simm's influence on "The Half-Breed";[17] nevertheless, the comparison is instructive: Whitman's Boddo is more aligned with contemporaneous half-blood characters created by such southern writers as Simms, who makes Goggle objectify the typically southern fear of miscegenation, than with those created by most northern writers, who (despite a prevalent ambivalence) more freely explore the meaning and the symbolic possibilities of the mixed-blood Indian.

Flint, Bird, and Whitman represent, as it were, a minority report from the eastern United States. Their regional contemporaries, while characteristically ambivalent, were more prepared to attempt less restricted portraits of the half-blood. To be sure, even these writers polarized toward white values; but frequently they focused on the positive and sometimes on the symbolic integral function of the half-blood, even when this function conflicted with their inherited cultural prejudice. Edward Willett is typical. In Bill Beeler's Bonanza (1892) he depicts Richard Le Breux, a Canadian half-blood, as a carousing trapper given to various vices, including gambling and scalping; yet Le Breux always remains a loyal friend to Bill Beeler. In Silver-spur (1870) Willett portrays Kate Robinette, the half-blood daughter of a trapper, during acts of savage violence when on several occasions she wields a battle axe against her enemies. Yet eventually she marries the protagonist of the novel, Fred Wilder, although, significantly, she first receives a substantial inheritance. Later, we are assured, in St. Louis "no one who was not acquainted with her story would have supposed that the greater part of her life had been spent among savages." [18]

Few, however, went as far as Oliver Gloux, the "French Cooper," whose *The White Scalper* (1881) presents a plot-facilitating half-blood named Lanzi, a minor Texan character who is an unequivocally brave, "loyal and devoted fellow." [19] Gloux benefited from a foreigner's exemption from American cultural ambivalence toward the half-blood, as did his fellow countrymen Tocqueville and Chateaubriand (whose *Les Natchez* [1826] includes a benign minor portrait of the offspring of a red-white marriage). In "Orso: An American Hercules" (1879), however, Henryk Sienkiewicz, an emigré Pole who spent more than a year in California before returning to Europe, presents an ugly half-blood misfit whose "powerful form looks like something hewn out with a hatchet" and whose presence makes animals cringe. [20] But Orso's "evil" appearance has less to do with any American convention than with the beauty-and-the-beast theme of the story; for Orso falls in love with an angelic blond beauty, saves her from a beating (with erotic overtones) by the director of the circus in which they are both performers, murders the director and four blacks, flees to the desert which his "Indian's instinct" converts into a benign refuge, and is taken in by a friendly squatter, with whom he and his wife live happily for the rest of their lives.

The prevalent pattern in the fiction of nineteenth-century eastern America is, interestingly, anticipated in a letter written on 21 December 1808 by Thomas Jefferson, who saw beyond the stereotypic notions evident in much of the subsequent fiction of his region and who in so many ways expressed the best of the southern mind. Addressed to the Delawares, Mohicans, and Munries, Jefferson's letter advises the Indians to abandon hunting and warfare for cultivation of the earth, which will lead to the need for the laws of white civilization to protect property and life, which in turn will integrate the declining red race with the advancing white race: "You will mix with us by marriage, your blood will run in our veins, and will spread with us over this great island." [21] In Jefferson's view white civilization is superior to red barbarism, and the white race can serve as a redemptive vehicle for the red race. Jefferson's benign outlook on miscegenation between the two races was shared by most of the nineteenth-century eastern writers, who treated the subject of racial intermarriage more liberally than did their southern contemporaries (Jefferson notwithstanding).

This context, however, is sometimes mute, as in *Hope Leslie* (1827) by Catherine Maria Sedgwick, the daughter of a racially tolerant Massachusetts family. In the novel Faith Leslie, who is modelled after the historical Eunice Williams,[22] is captured by Indians and eventually adopts their language and customs. She is hated by the Puritan colonists and she seldom appears in the novel; but Sedgwick clearly presents Faith's decision to marry Oneco and to spend her life as a member of his tribe as a viable option.

Miscegenation between the two races is treated similarly in Lydia Maria Child's *Hobomok* (1824), in which Mary Conant falls in love with a Pequod Indian "cast in nature's noblest mould."[23] A loyal agent for the Salem residents of 1692, Hobomok has lost his primitive fierceness. Reflecting upon the Indian's service, Mary's father confesses, "I have sat by the hour together, and gazed on his well-fared face, till the tears have come into mine eyes, that the Lord should have raised us up so good a friend, among the savages" (pp. 122–23); but when he learns of Mary's marriage to Hobomok, he says he prefers her to be dead (p. 166). Mary, who is somewhat rebellious toward the voice of social authority, not only marries Hobomok but also bears him a son.

The marriage is an extremely good one until Charles Brown, to whom Mary had previously been betrothed and whom rumor reported to have drowned years ago, returns. He too had rebelled against Salem authority by heretically embracing Episcopalianism, and so he fictively makes a good mate for Mary. When "kind, noble-hearted" Hobomok learns of Brown's return, he broken-heartedly decides to free Mary from her marriage to him and to disappear into the West, thereby permitting the two former lovers to wed. "Be kind to my boy," he instructs Brown, who in turn assures him, "He shall be my own boy" (pp. 175, 186).

Child may imply the superiority of the marriage between white and white over that between red and white,[24] but intellectually she does not condemn miscegenation or its offspring. She presents the half-blood boy as an ordinary child readily integrated among white youth: "Now he would be wholly concealed behind his mother's dress, and now, one roguish black eye would slily peep out upon his favorite companion, the laughing little Mary Collier" (p. 187). Moreover, Mary's father abandons his hostility toward the child, as "little Hobomok was always a peculiar favorite with his grandfather" (p. 187). Most significant, Child tells us at the conclusion of her book that little Hobomok, whose mixed blood symbolizes the new emergent American strain, eventually became "a distinguished graduate at Cambridge" and even studied in England (p. 187).

Child's credentials on the subject of race relations are good ones. In *Letters from New-York* (1843) she admits a spiritual and physical difference between the red and the white race, "but it is as the difference between trees of the same forest, not as between trees and minerals"; and in "The Quadroons" (1846), she dramatizes the tragic effect of white social reaction to tainted blood on an innocent woman who becomes a raving maniac when she learns of her Negro ancestry and of her own destiny as a slave.[25] Yet a certain ambivalence tugs at Child's conscious message about miscegenation in *Hobomok;* this message, particularly as objectified in the half-blood, is undermined by Child's instinctive allegiance to the values of white society, with its fear of taint. Consequently the Indian side of the younger Hobomok must recede even as his father sacrificially retreats before Brown and white civilization. Not only is the young half-blood fully integrated into white social values, but, Child tells us in the final words of the book, "His father was seldom spoken of; and by degrees his Indian appellation was silently omitted" (pp. 187–88). This concluding remark inadvertently repudiates Child's conscious intention in her portraits of the older Hobomok as a "noble savage" and of the younger Hobomok as symbolic of an invigorated, emergent American race.

A less benign example of eastern sentiment toward miscegenation is expressed in a novel by James Kirke Paulding, the Jeffersonian New Yorker best known for his collaboration with Washington and William Irving on *Salmagundi* (1807–1808). In his mischievous *Koningsmarke, the Long Finne* (1823), Paulding has a black witch, a slave named Bombie, transform Jefferson's vision into a prophecy of dire consequences: "Yes, yes, ye proud, upstart race, the time shall surely come, when the pile of oppression ye have reared to the clouds shall fall, and crush your own heads. Black men and red men, all colours, shall combine against your pale, white race; and the children of the masters shall become the bondsmen of the posterity of the slave."[26] This threat of racial amalgamation and vengeance, including the possibility that rampant miscegenation could engulf the white race, informs, as we have seen, the curse of Simms's witch a little over ten years later. But Simms's message in *The Partisan* is antithetical to Paulding's in the passage cited, which implicitly argues *against* slavery and racial prejudice.

Although neither Paulding's nor Sedgwick's novel depicts a half-blood and although Child's novel presents him very briefly, each typically illustrates a tolerance (however ambivalent) toward miscegenation among many eastern American writers in the early part of the century, a tolerance defining the context in which half-blood characters appear in the fiction of their regional contemporaries. In fact this liberal disposition emerges even earlier in Susanna Hoswell Rowson's *Reuben and Rachel* (1798), a wretchedly mismanaged novel published two years outside the perimeter of my study but which is included because of its instructive value. A hodge-podge of history, legends, Indian captivity narratives, Gothic motifs, and sentimental tradition, Rowson's novel presents a complicated genealogical account tracing intermarriages between the red and white race as far back as Columbus's discovery of the New World. At the end of an incredibly boring first volume, Reuben and Rachel are born. They are twin progeny of Reuben Dudley, who possesses a "dark complexion, the nature of his father's marriage with [Indian] Oberea, which in law would have been termed illegal," and Cassiah Penn, whose face is "not so fair as to be pale, nor dark enough to be termed brown; it was a beautiful [half-blood-like] mixture of the white rose and [red] carnation that glowed on her forehead, tinted her cheeks, and gave animation to her dark hazel eyes."[27] Rowson never flinches during her narration of abundant miscegenation, for she views these New World intermarriages as symbolic of the animation and vigor indigenous to emerging America, which had just consummated its independence on 3 September 1783 (when the treaty with Britain was signed), only fifteen years before the publication of her novel. In an early episode, for instance, a white man describes his marriage to an Indian maiden as "the cement to bind them [the two races] in bonds of lasting amity"

(p. 158), a remark doubtless based on Rolfe's reasoning in his marriage to Pocahontas. In Rowson's novel, this bond defines the distinctive vigor underlying America's half-blood-like superiority to the Old World.

Rowson's angle of vision is indeed Jeffersonian in the fullest sense; for she carefully indicates that such intermarriages, whatever their broad symbolism and vague mutual benefits, result in the elevation of the red race and do not lower or imperil the white race. Consequently, in spite of the fact that mixed-blood Reuben has mingled with Indians and has attracted the affections of a half-blood squaw named Eumea (who has saved his life), he "had seen too much of savage men and manners to have a wish to remain amongst them, even though he might have been elevated to the highest seat of dignity" (p. 295), even though, we might add, he could marry Eumea. Eumea is described as "a dear creature, who, though she is a little darkish or so, has a heart as beautiful as an angel." Having benefited from Reuben's civilized instruction, she "assiduously endeavoured to conform to the European dress, customs and manners" (pp. 351, 354). Reuben, however, does not polarize toward the Indian side of his dual heritage, so Eumea is rejected by him, her fulfillment of the Jeffersonian prophecy denied. There is no discernible reason why Rowson permitted this inconsistency, so palpably in conflict with the events depicted in the first volume of her novel. She simply has Eumea conveniently commit suicide by drowning, thereby sacrificially freeing Reuben to marry Jeffy Oliver. Whereas Eumea was, as a manifestation of the savage side of her nature and of her tribal identity, prone to "the most violent affliction" of impetuosity, Jeffy is a sedate young woman of English parentage who excels in the performance of "every elegant domestic employment" (pp. 195, 354). Half-blood Eumea may be "the sweetest of the savages" (p. 361), but finally only restrained, decorous Jeffy is, for Rowson, the proper model for the novel's adolescent female audience. The reader must be satisfied with the detail that Eumea had been secretly loved by a character named O'Neil, who never loved again; but the gap between the image of the half-blood as a symbol for the new American identity in the first volume and Reuben's repudiation of his Indian side in the second volume, among other narrative defects, rends Rowson's novel. This disparity between authorial intention and execution is a recurrent feature in the fiction with half-blood characters written by eastern authors during the nineteenth century.

This conflict appears in many guises, even in works published late in the century, when the fictional half-blood was more freely romanticized because his real-life counterpart was less palpably menacing on a frontier already vanishing. In *Ramona* (1884), for instance, Helen Hunt Jackson depicts a remarkably beautiful half-blood heroine. While thinking of Ramona's "mongrel blood," her foster mother, Señora Morena, wishes the child had at least been a pure blood Indian: "I like not these crosses. It is the worst, and not the best of each, that remains." She is certain that Ramona will evince "the instincts of her nature," that "the Indian blood in [her] veins would show someday."[28] When Ramona learns of her mixed blood, she is not overwhelmed (as frequently is the case), for it supports her attachment to Alessandro, a full-blood Indian who she eventually marries. But Ramona is not exempt from problems of identity. Her dual heritage suspends her between the Spanish and Indian cultures, both receding in the novel before the inhumane advance of white American civilization. She is, in Señora Morena's opinion, too good to marry an Indian and not good enough to marry Spanish gentry (literally, Filipe, the Señora's son).

But in the novel Ramona emerges as an ideal mate for both; and after Alessandro is mistakenly murdered as a horse thief, Ramona eventually weds Filipe and moves with him from California to Mexico. These concluding acts in the novel suggest the demise of the Indian in America and the withdrawal of Spanish presence in the West, both of which Jackson presents as a genuine loss. But of the two, the Spanish world is presented more realistically and forcefully, a fact which in time disturbed Jackson, who had intended the novel to dramatize the numerous injustices inflicted on the dispossessed Indians in the West.[29] Jackson, a New Englander who spent only a total of eleven months in California, could not make her Indian characters ring true. Alessandro is said to be but is never shown to be an uncivilized man with "only single, primitive, uneducated instincts and impressions" (p. 63); and "a gentler, sweeter maiden never drew breath than" Ramona (p. 107). In order to make them sympathetic characters, Jackson presented them as romantic figures of the sort her white audience expected. In effect, Ramona is a half-blood in name only. That she should finally side with her Spanish heritage, the dominant force in the novel, and that she should move to Mexico illustrate Jackson's unconscious retreat from the reality of the red race as a dispossessed culture in the West and from the reality of the Indian side of the novel's half-blood heroine.

Two years earlier Mayne Reid's *The Wild Huntress* (1882) appeared, featuring two "stunning" heroines whose mother was a half-blood. Marion and Lillian Holt are, of course, quarter-bloods, though their antagonist, a full-blood Chicasaw woman, speaks of them as half-bloods. Their recessive Indian taint permits Reid to stress that the sisters are "more white than Injun," an emphasis which in turn allows him to present them as heroines who are as radiant as any pure white equivalent in the sentimental fiction of the period.[30] On the whole, however, Reid's work does not reveal intensified modes of the tension we have been discussing, doubtless because he was a European who spent only a small part of his life in midwestern and eastern America. Reid benefited from an outsider's perspective on the half-blood, as did Sienkiewicz, Tocqueville, Chateaubriand, and Gloux. His *The White Squaw* (1883), in fact, presents an educated half-blood Seminole chief as its heroic protagonist. "Remarkably handsome," Wacora's "soul was Indian" and "his soul was noble—his heart pure."[31] When he meets Alice Rody, a pure white, he loses interest in Sansuta, the Indian maiden of whom he had been enamoured; and Alice falls in love with him, reflecting on "his intelligence, chivalric courage, and purity of thought" (p. 18). Wacora, "the noble savage[,] was ready to sacrifice himself for her [Alice's] welfare" (p. 22), but it is Sansuta who conveniently dies. Alice marries Wacora at the end of the novel and (*mirabile dictu*) lives with him among the Indians. Sansuta's death by no means foreshadows the demise of the Indians in general and of the Indian side of Wacora in particular; it simply facilitates the plot of the novel. Though Reid is apparently exempt from American cultural antagonism toward such an ending, he does offer a rationale of sorts when he has Alice think that it might be better had Wacora been raised in white society but that, in the final analysis, white civilization tended toward its own forms of barbarism, whence she leaves her white family and friends forever without a qualm.

More typical than Reid's *The White Squaw* is "The Alien" (1907) by John G. Neihardt, an early twentieth-century author who spent most of his life in Illinois and Nebraska. "The Alien" suffers from an unresolved conflict between Neihardt's portrait of the story's half-blood protagonist as "more beast than man" and his criticism of hostile social attitudes toward Antoine, who is "an outcast, a man of no race."[32] Neihardt presents Antoine as a murderer and a horse-thief with "a face of bestial malevolence," as a social misfit in the red and the white race, and as a rejected son of his Indian mother. Turned away by the father of a woman he loves, he kills the man, is hunted by a posse, and befriends a she-wolf, whom he names after the lost Susette. In dialectic with the malignity of Antoine is the sympathy we are to feel over this utter loneliness, over the fact that as a bastard and a half-blood he "hain't got no people" (pp. 126, 127) among whom he can express his need for love. At the end of the story even the she-wolf, with whom he has been sleeping, betrays him; while he is feverishly ill, she brings a male wolf with her into the cave and, when Antoine is about to overcome the attacking male, she fatally bites him in the throat. By the end of the story it is impossible to say whether Antoine is more beast than man because of his illegitimate half-blood nature or because of social ostracism which has driven him from the realm of humanity to the world of beasts, where he is also a misfit. Neihardt seems to seek our sympathy for Antoine's plight, but he dramatizes the half-blood's malevolence more forcefully than its probable social cause, with the result that the story's conclusion seems more just than sad.

Neihardt's ambivalence toward Antoine was anticipated in the fiction of Edward S. Ellis, a New Jersey schoolteacher. In *The Hunter Hunted* (1880) and in *Scar-Cheek, the Wild Half-Breed* (1909), the mixed-blood Indian is a vindictive villain given to dissipation and vicious self-indulgence, whereas in *The Half-Blood* (1882) his portrait is more complex.[33] Kaam, the son of an English father and an Arapaho mother, experiences an identity crisis emanating from the conflict between his highly refined education and his murky disposition. When he discovers that he is a half-blood and that Harry Harmer is not his real father, Kaam reels "as if stricken a blow," and a "moody melancholy . . . settle[s] upon him" (p. 10). He now begins to comprehend why, in his youth, "he sometimes

thought it strange that distinctions had been made between himself and others": "Raised in civilized society and instructed by education in its distinctions, he felt that he, the half-breed, son of a
father who had previously married, and whose wife and loyal offspring still lived, held but a questionable place among those with
whom he had mingled; and fancying himself, as it were, in an am-
phitheater, gazed upon by the assembled world, who all were possessed of his story, he shrunk from the gaze of human eyes" (p. 10).
Compounding his problem is the disclosure that his real father
had murdered Kaam's mother and had planned to sell his mixed-
blood son as a slave, painful facts aggravated by the apparent loss
of his lover, Julia Severance, to Adolph Murtel, the all-white son
of Kaam's father.

Ellis suggests that prejudicial social attitudes to some extent
account for the increasing withdrawal of Kaam's refined or civilized
characteristics: "To be honorable, of pure birth, and respected parentage, was . . . to be born heir to the right rule, and to lack these
requisites was to hold a place among the common multitude—
earth's crowd—which great minds live to control, scourge when
they rebel, and which they drive to toil like the cattle of the fields"
(p. 10). Ellis seems sympathetic to Kaam's newly aroused contempt
for "the whole system of civilization, under which such destruction
could exist, or such wrongs be perpetuated"; and this social injustice
contributes to the emergence of Kaam's primitive heritage, for now
"the Indian in his nature was fully awakened" (p. 11). With no
place in civilization Kaam leaves for the wilderness, the "savage
grandeur" of which seizes "upon the enthusiasm of his nature" (p.
11) and apparently releases the potential for savagery threateningly
lurking within the half-blood's self.

For some time Kaam finds contentment as a chief of the Arapaho
until Adolph Murtel reappears. Kaam resists an impulse to slay
his adversary (for Julia's sake, he thinks); but this vestige of his
civilized self gives way when he learns that Murtel has deserted
Julia after she became pregnant with Murtel's child and that he
has subsequently slandered her. Now Kaam seeks "dearest revenge"
by saving Murtel from death on several occasions only to lure him
into a sense of security, which suddenly vanishes one day when
Kaam reveals his identity and slits his captive's veins, resulting in
the slow death of his adversary. There is, to be sure, "justice" in

this murderous vengeance, but irresolution characterizes Ellis's management of Kaam's polarization toward his Indian heritage. The atoning death of Kaam's pure-white half-brother is followed by the dissolution of the half-blood's relation to the white race: Julia dies before he can rescue her from despair, and Harry Harmer, his surrogate father, also perishes—"every tie which bound Kaam to the whites was severed" (p. 15). In his final appearance in the novel, Kaam bravely and successfully defends the Arapaho from attacking Pawnees; and "the once proud-hearted half-breed, whose aspirations, under the influence of civilization, had been all refined, now stood among this wild tribe, with gory knife and human trophies, an acknowledged *savage*!" (p. 15). But, Ellis adds, Kaam does not enjoy his triumph, even though he lives with his mother (who, we learn, had not been slain after all), and he compulsively hates white people: "A settled gloom hangs on his brow, and his people no longer call him *Kaam*, or 'Daylight,' but *MoKah*, or 'Night'" (p. 15). Kaam's divided nature admits no easy resolution, a problem related to Ellis's uncertainty (similar to Neihardt's) whether white social injustice or latent red savagery better accounts for Kaam's movement towards primitivism. Clearly Kaam's identification with his Indian heritage is the easier of the two alternatives Ellis entertains, and clearly this outcome obviates Ellis's ambivalence toward his half-blood character.

Somewhat more successful management occurs in William Manning's *Texas Chick, the Southwest Detective* (1884), which presents a half-blood maid named Moza. Walter Latimer, a Virginian, is amorously attracted to Moza, and he finds her both beautiful and "unusually intelligent for one of her mixed blood."[34] The villain of the story, a Mexican assassin named Pedro Lopez, says that Moza's "blood is bad and false" (p. 5); but of course Moza's character is really virtuous. Moza benefits from the gentler treatment which half-blood women, in contrast to their brothers, *generally* received in fact and in fiction during the century. Ironically, however, all Moza's good qualities are measured against an alleged pejorative norm for her hybrid race; all of her remarkable qualities are exceptional for a half-blood, and therein Manning's ambivalence toward Moza's "Indian taint" (p. 16) is revealed. This dubiety is further evidenced in the fact that at the novel's conclusion Latimer marries Florence Riverton, the outlaw queen driven to a life among desperadoes by "bitter wrongs" (p. 25) but redeemed from that life by the revengeful death of Lopez. Moza, not quite worthy of the hero, is conveniently wedded to an unnamed person.

Equally instructive are the novels of the deutero-Edward L. Wheeler. In Wheeler's fiction, half-bloods of every sort can be found, ranging from an unnamed member of an "evil-faced and brutal looking" gang of outlaws in *Bob Woolf, the Border Ruffian* (1899)[35] to White Eagle, "the Handsome Half-breed," in *Sierra Sam, the Detective* (1900). Wheeler's need to assure his readers that White Eagle evinces "nothing but a dusky tinge of countenance to denote that Indian blood coursed through his veins," that "he was in a better sense a white man, possessed of education, intellect and honor," discloses an authorial ambivalence tugging at the portrait of the half-blood as "well known through the whole territory and well spoken of." White Eagle survives his enemies by disguising himself as a Jew, as a member of another racial group looked upon with suspicion by white settlers in the West.[36] Wheeler's ambivalence, however, is most pronounced in *Nobby Nick of Nevada* (1899), in which the daughter of a half-blood named Stern Face reflects white society's views—Wheeler's unconscious views—even though she has always been confined to the wilderness and to Indian ways. "Though a half-breed, he [Stern Face] received an excellent education," she explains to Nick, the novel's protagonist; "My father has been my instructor, and to him I owe such knowledge as I have not learned from experience and reading. Though the taint of Indian blood is in my veins, my heart is as white and my education nearly as perfect as that of my white sister."[37] She seems to praise her father, but the qualifications "though a half-breed" and "though the taint of Indian blood is in my veins" violate the credulity of her characterization by unwittingly revealing Wheeler's dubiety over the issue of mixed-bloods. Nevertheless, the daughter's clearly defined recessive Indian "taint" and her sense of "distance" from the half-blood condition of her father permit Wheeler to allow Nick to marry her by the end of the novel.

Among the most interesting examples of the tension between authorial intention and execution is William Snelling's *Tales of the Northwest* (1830), a very neglected literary work of the American frontier. Snelling's work suffers from various aesthetic limitations and disproportions of the sort which irritate some contemporary critical sensibilities, so the book is seldom mentioned other than in literary histories.[38] Nevertheless, Snelling's volume is, in my opinion, significant in ways as yet undisclosed by critical commentary; it is not only a noteworthy classic of the Old Northwest but also a fascinating documentation of cultural conflict with important artistic ramifications. Explicitly, *Tales of the Northwest* relates numerous details about early nineteenth-century frontier life, but of greater interest to the student of American culture is the work's implicit revelation of a disparity between Snelling's intent and his achievement, between attempted imaginative design and the resistance of literary convention. This tension alerts us to certain peculiar problems confronting the artist of the frontier, especially when treating the half-blood, and also functions as a dynamic feature in Snelling's book.

Conflict within the work has not been entirely overlooked. One critic has observed that despite Snelling's expressed intention to describe Indian life apart from any theory, he in fact uses civilization as a measure of the differences between the cultures and thereby demonstrates that "savage gifts are gifts of loss."[39] This observation is correct as far as it goes; what warrants further scrutiny is the degree to which this conflict arises from a deeper cultural and artistic stress in the work, from the emergence of specific aspects of the ambivalence Snelling and his contemporaries felt when they depicted the frontier. In *Tales of the Northwest* this ambivalence particularly surfaces in Snelling's search for a character who will adequately represent and dramatize the indigenous qualities of the Old Northwest, a search complicated by his fundamental distrust of most of the types of humanity he encountered on the frontier.

Snelling attempted a tenuous compromise in his portrait of a half-blood, but lurking in the background was still another conflict, the problem presented by the absence of a literary vehicle appropriate for his half-blood protagonist. Snelling fared less well with this difficulty, for while he tried in his portrait of the half-blood to resolve his ambivalence over the encounter of the red and white cultures, the creative impulse informing this reconciliation was thwarted by an artistic problem: the unavailability of any contemporary literary form to embody the significance of the integration of races symbolized by the half-blood.

At one level, Snelling's sketches depict the collision of the red and white races on the frontier; the very first tale may in fact be read as the epitome of this encounter. "The Captive" concerns two distinctive modes of justice: the Indian's sense of "an eye for an eye" and the pioneer's sense of civil law. In a postscript to the story, Snelling explicitly deplores the "evils attendant" on this difference (p. 23), a point dramatized as well in "The Devoted."[40] But, as his introductory remarks indicate, Snelling wishes to de-emphasize the differences between the two races and to reveal the essential similarities between them. "There are wise and good men among Indians, but they are few and far apart, as in civilized nations, and about in the same proportion to their numbers," Snelling explains, adding that "They have as many of the vices and follies of human nature as other people, and it is believed no more" (p. 4). The significant feature of these comments is less Snelling's use of civilization as a standard for measuring Indian life than his scrutiny of a fundamental agreement between the races. Snelling's intention to depict this congruence informs his search in the book for characters who reflect an integration of the races.

Sometimes Snelling responds to the apparent conflict between the two cultures by avoiding the issue altogether, as in those sketches focused exclusively on Indian protagonists performing entirely within an Indian context. These tales, however, are not as elaborately developed or narrated as others involving both races; presumably their origin in legends or accounts narrated second-hand intimidates Snelling, who exercises restraint over his presentation of them. Snelling appears to be somewhat more engaged, at the level of authorial management of his material, in those sketches portraying characters who in some fashion join the two cultures. "Charles Hess," for instance, concerns a white man who lives on the frontier, marries an Indian, fathers half-blood children, and in several respects combines something of civilization and something of the wilderness in his life style. "Pinchon," too, recounts the exploits of a "white savage" (p. 214); and "Weenokhenchah Wandeeteekah," ostensibly a story about an Indian, depicts its protagonist as a fop of the forest (Snelling's phrase) with "a skin lighter by five shades than the natural complexion of the Dahcotahs" (p. 170). These stories may have a legendary or folk tale basis, but their presentation evinces more authorial interaction with the narration than do most of the "pure" Indian sketches. By depicting characters who unite features of both civilization and wilderness, these works certainly come closer to fulfilling Snelling's aim to portray fundamental affinities between the red and white races.

Even in these tales, however, Snelling fails to find a character who satisfactorily reconciles the conflict between the races and who demonstrates their essential harmony. His most successful attempt appears in "The Bois Brûlé," by far the longest story in *Tales of the Northwest* (nearly one hundred pages in the Flanagan edition), the only sketch in the book divided into chapters, and the work placed exactly at the center of the volume. The work is a short novel, and when compared to the other, slighter tales, it emerges as the narrative in which Snelling has demonstrably most invested himself as an artist.

Snelling's view of half-bloods, the result of his nearly eight years in the Old Northwest, reflects the ambivalence typical of his eastern contemporaries. But in the pivotal "The Bois Brûlé" he tries to reconcile cultural conflicts in William Gordon, tries to make his half-blood protagonist representative of a new race emerging on the frontier. Of this hybrid race, in general, Snelling writes: "The half-breeds of the North-west are physically a fine race of men. The mixture of blood seems an improvement on the Indian and white. By it, the muscular strength of the one, and the easy grace, and power of endurance of the other, are blended" (p. 78). The Indian feature of Gordon's nature accounts for his equestrian skills (praised by the Hohays, p. 99), his possession of "an uncommon share" of physical prowess (p. 136), and his overall stamina and daring. That same side accounts for the fact that he is "subject to sudden starts of passion" (p. 88), for one very distinctive characteristic of the Indian, according to Snelling and others, is an inconsistency and caprice dictated by passion (p. 5). The civilized component of Gordon, on the other hand, explains why at times his "red kindred" think he is deceived by the "foolish notions" of the white race (pp. 102, 103), why he is educated (he attended the Catholic Seminary in Quebec, where he suffered from prejudice), articulate, and able in one episode to organize a large number of aroused half-bloods (p. 139).

Snelling experienced difficulty in sustaining his integration of the red and white races in Gordon. Like his eastern contemporaries,

he found the "fine race" of mixed-blood Indians emotionally trou-
blesome. When, in a minor moment in the story, he refers to "the
erratic half breeds" (p. 105), he reveals a certain irresolution concerning his use of Gordon as a symbol of the benign possibility
of a synthetic race emerging from racial conflict on the frontier.
Snelling might have been able to maintain his integration had he
not unconsciously run into another difficulty, a problem related
to the fact that, as one critic remarked, "As long as Eastern romantic standards prevailed, there would be in the West a kind of bastard
literature, a grafting of the scenic effects of the West to the senti-
mentality of the East, and a resultant absurd distortion."[41] Specifically, Snelling's "new" protagonist in American fiction—a character uniting the extremes of the American experience on the frontier and to some extent suspending American dubiousness toward
this experience—required a suitable literary vehicle. But because
he found no model and because he lacked sufficient artistic ingenu-
ity to create one, Snelling relied on the formulae of the conventional sentimental novel of his time, a dependence eventually sub-
verting his central intention in making a half-blood the protagonist
of the story.

The most evident effect of the insufficiency of the literary vehicle is the mutation of Gordon's character as the story develops.
At the beginning of the tale, Snelling tends to emphasize the Indian
attributes of Gordon's nature, his vigorous and boldly heroic qualities. From the first through the seventh chapters, Gordon typically
saves Flora and Duncan Cameron from death in a frozen lake; out-
wits and kills LaVerdure, a Canadian who intended to eat the *métis;*
saves a Sioux woman from the wrath of the Hohays; and participates
in a reckless buffalo hunt. At the end of this hunt, Flora, who
has been sprayed with the blood of a slain animal, faints; and
Gordon springs from his horse, snatches a cup, runs to a hole in
a frozen stream, and in less than two minutes returns to sprinkle
water on the face of the reviving Flora (whose first word, as sentimental tradition would have it, is the pronunciation of his name).
Immediately following this episode and concluding the seventh
chapter, Gordon contends with two Indians who have attacked
Flora's father; during the ensuing battle the half-blood is wounded.
From this point onward, Snelling, who by means of the wound has
in effect limited his protagonist's ability to continue reckless feats

of physical prowess, increasingly demonstrates Gordon's heroic activities in terms of more civilized gallantry and mores. Significantly, at the end of the story, when Gordon has captured M'Leod (who slew the half-blood's good friend, Cavenny), he does not yield to the sort of passion for revenge the Indian side of his nature requires and that in the earlier part of the tale would have predominated. He now spares his adversary's life, and, curiously, is dubious about his own motivation: "His expectations were near being fulfilled: Gordon's men, who had watched the duel with intense curiosity, now levelled their weapons, and would have shot him, had not the bois brulé called to them to forbear. 'Wretch,' he cried, 'I scarcely know what hinders me from staking you to the earth'" (pp. 164–65). What prevents Gordon is the dominance of the civilized part of his nature, that part emphasized over the Indian half in the second part of the story. Snelling, it seems, has been (perhaps unconsciously) transforming his protagonist into a suitable spouse for Flora, who, we are told, "was such a maiden, in appearance at least, as the novelists of the last century usually took for a heroine" (p. 86). This is a revealing remark; in conjunction with its implicit indication of Snelling's refusal to create a fresh character in Flora, it suggests the degree to which the formulae of the sentimental novel, with its European heritage, have had a grip on the story from the first. This conventional fictional model distorts Snelling's portrait of the half-blood, who, with unhappy frequency in the second half of the story, is referred to as "our hero." In fact, the thrust of this convention, as representatively embodied in Flora, forces Snelling to bifurcate his protagonist in spite of the fact that he was originally designed to integrate, as a member of a hybrid race, both Indian strength and civilized grace.

This split results in another instructive change in the story. At precisely the point where Gordon revives Flora and shortly thereafter receives a wound, Snelling introduces another half-blood, Antoine Dés Champs, who becomes Gordon's *Doppelgänger* and who (like the faithful confidante prevalent in sentimental novels[42]) never leaves the side of the protagonist until the end of the story. At one point we are told of his assistance to Gordon that "a brother could not have tended him with more attention than did Dés Champs" (p. 148). Whereas previously Gordon performed his feats alone, he now does everything with Dés Champs, who accompanies him while others hesitate or refuse (pp. 143, 148). In fact, even the final deliverance of Flora is achieved by both half-bloods rather than by Gordon alone (p. 157). As the second half of the story develops, Dés Champs increasingly serves as the repository of Gordon's Indian talents, which are being displaced by the civilized features of the protagonist's nature. Not only does Dés Champs possess uncommon physical powers of the sort initially ascribed to Gordon—e.g., "he was the swiftest runner of the north-west" (p. 140)—but, significantly, he insists on the natural conclusion to Gordon's revengeful hunt for M'Leod. Whereas Gordon, to his own apparent surprise, refuses to kill M'Leod and thereby express the passionate Indian side of his nature prevalent at the start of the story, Dés Champs, accompanying him as usual, ties the captive's "wrists so tight as to give him great pain, for it must be confessed that the half-breed, as well as others of his rank and condition, had little regard for human suffering" (p. 165). Gordon, however, loosens the bonds, angering Dés Champs (who typically views pain from the Indian perspective delineated throughout Snelling's book) to the point where he complains, "If·I were master, I would not have all this trouble with them"; he would "carry home their scalps at my horse's bridle" (p. 165).

But Dés Champs is not the master, even as the Indian features of Gordon have become subordinate to the forces of civilization in his nature. Appropriately, by the end of the tale, the Indians no longer think of Gordon as a kinsman but identify him with the white race (p. 151). Equally fitting is the Earl of Selkirk's reference to "the gallantry" of Gordon, "who, he said, had fairly won her [Flora] in the fashion of the days of chivalry" (p. 161). Indeed by the end of the story Gordon has become the chivalrous rustic common to the sentimental novel.[43]

The image evoked by the Earl recalls the European tradition of Snelling's literary vehicle, and in fact Europe actually becomes Gordon's final home. In accord with a convention of many sentimental novels, Gordon, who now manifests only his white heritage, is showered with riches.[44] He subsequently not only moves East but eventually crosses the Atlantic to reside "on the banks of the Esk" (p. 168). Before leaving the Old Northwest, however, he encourages Dés Champs to accompany him. But the dichotomy is virtually complete, and Dés Champs refuses to go, revealingly suggesting that the capriciousness of the Indian side of his nature is responsible for the decision (p. 166)—an explanation intimating the degree to which Dés Champs has become the repository of Gordon's Indian heritage. This Indian heritage is again stressed when, in the same scene, Dés Champs, "a total stranger to the delicacy which would have made many white men refuse such a gift" (p. 167), asks for and takes Gordon's horse and gun. These last vestiges of Gordon's Indian heritage having been removed and now associated with Dés Champs, Snelling's protagonist is completely transformed into the "our hero" of the sentimental novel; he is now a quite suitable spouse for Flora, whom (we should remember) Snelling described as a conventional heroine of the sort found in such fiction.

There may have been other reasons why Snelling's ambivalence toward mixed-blood Indians and the limitations of his literary vehicle subverted his design in Gordon. The book contains hints that a real end to the conflict between the red and white races is not likely without (as Snelling's experience on the frontier seemed to indicate) the destruction of the Indians. This sense of their probable annihilation may well have been one of the motivating energies behind Snelling's attempt to record the Indians as they really were; but it is certainly localized in his postscript about Dés Champs, who now embodies Gordon's red heritage. While Gordon goes on to enjoy life with a sizable family in Europe, Dés Champs dies very soon after Gordon's departure. His death during a buffalo hunt not only suggests Snelling's ambivalence about life on the frontier but intimates his intuition about the eventual elimination of the wilderness and, with it, of the Indian.

Elsewhere in the book, he speaks of the advancements of communication in the Old Northwest in terms that suggest the extinction of the Indian: "The breath of civilization has at length blown away all obstacles. Steam has conquered the Father of Waters, to the astonishment of the savages and the terror of the catfishes" (p. 42). Equally pertinent are the last words of "The Bois Brulé" referring to the village around which the action of the story has largely centered: "At present it does not exist" (p. 169). Beyond ostensible conflict and beyond a wished-for reconciliation or integration, Snelling's book conveys a sense of a frontier slowly vanishing before the forces of civilization. We should perhaps recall that, like his protagonist, Snelling returned to the East, where he spent the rest of his life as a journalist and an editor.

A similar tension occurs in L. Augustus Jones's *Bloody Brook* (1866), in which the portrait of Villegrand, a half-blood villain, never achieves a balanced integration of his Indian and his civilized features. On the one hand, Villegrand is a twenty-five-year-old Mohegan chief evincing physical prowess and various masculine traits; on the other hand, his affection for Belle Bright (a white woman) frequently overpowers his masculinity, and he spends a goodly amount of his time lamenting and pining (reminiscent of certain female characters in the sentimental fiction of the day) after Belle rejects him as a suitor. Jones fails to integrate these two features of Villegrand, even though he attributes the half-blood's change of heart towards the white race and his own white heritage to Belle's rejection, and implies the transformation of the half-blood's civilized lore into savage passion. Villegrand threatens Belle, and when that fails to win her, he kidnaps her and makes war on her friends and acquaintances. For all his alleged ferocity, Villegrand still pines; and as the novel lengthens, the caricature of the half-blood remains distorted until finally his Indian side gains ascendancy. By the end of the novel Villegrand is thoroughly villainous, his white sentimental side virtually vanquished. The degree of degeneration which occurs can be assessed by contrasting his initial appearance as a vigorous affectionate youth with his final appearance as a fiendish savage who lacks redeeming civilized qualities. In this last scene, Jones writes, Villegrand's "garb hung in shreds about his form—his hair floated in wild disorder over his shoulders—the war paint mingling with the perspiration that streamed down his face, rendered his features frightfully hideous."[45] During his attempted escape he encounters a gaunt, half-famished dog (it is the settlers' lost dog!) which fatally attacks him "with savage fury" (p. 95), a fitting finish for a character who has relinquished his white heritage and gives way to "the savage . . . aroused within" him and to "wild love" (pp. 17, 96). Even this late in the novel, however, Jones tries once more to resurrect the white features of the half-blood. Through his heroine, Jones reminds us that Villegrand genuinely loved Belle, leaving us then with a confused, distorted impression rather than with a clear portrait of the half-blood. Exhibiting a civilized sense of love (even citing Scripture on the subject) as well as the primitive sway of passion, Villegrand is irresolvably and fatally divided against himself; and so, mercifully, he dies.

While Jones, Snelling, and Rowson unwittingly encounter in their novels a tension that subverts the development of their mixed-blood characters, Nathaniel Hawthorne and Herman Melville carefully focus on the very antitheses of the mixed-blood as indicative of an irremediable and fundamental bifurcation in the human self (even as Poe suggested through his half-blood character) and, apparently for Melville, even in the universe. The half-blood in Hawthorne's unfinished novel *Septimius Felton* (1872) is the protagonist's grandfather or great-grandfather (precisely which remains uncertain in the manuscript[46]) and he is mentioned only to provide Septimius with the taint of Indian blood. In *The Marble Faun* (1860) Hawthorne alludes to "a great deal of color" in Miriam's nature (possibly a trace of African ancestry) and in many of his writings, perhaps most notably in "Young Goodman Brown" and "The Maypole of Merrymount," he makes good use of an Indian motif to suggest the primitive, amoral, spontaneous side of the self, that feature repressed by "civilized" conscience, guilt and sorrow. But only in *Septimius Felton*, probably written sometime between 1855 and 1861, does he actually depict this contrast in a mixed-blood character. Septimius, like so many of Hawthorne's central characters, is at war with himself, and (reminiscent of a device used by Poe in "The Fall of the House of Usher" and by Melville in *Moby-Dick*) his brow is said to evince "a very deep furrow or corrugation, or fissure, it might almost be called" (p. 116). Sharing in "the customary American abhorrence for any mixture of blood" (p. 141), Septimius unconsciously seeks to repudiate his taint—"the wild natural blood of the Indian, the instinctive, the animal nature" (p. 188). To this end he exerts his rational powers excessively in order to master and control nature, specifically to use nature to achieve immortality and thereby assert the dominance of spirit (white civilized reason) over flesh (red primitive instinct). Although the Indian blood in him is "diluted, and modified likewise by higher civilization," Septimius is subject to the "same tendency" as his aunt, whose "savage strain . . . sometimes snatch[es] her back into barbarian life and its instincts" (p. 88); so his unnatural aspiration is doomed from the outset. In Hawthorne's view, the two strains of blood represent the spontaneous joy and the restraining guilt or sorrow which characterize the extremes of the human self and in fact define the very dynamics of that self, a mixture of flesh and spirit, emotion and reason, community and isolation. In this sense, Hawthorne seems to suggest, we are all mixed-bloods; and rather than attempt to negate one or the other side of our dual heritage, we ought to learn, like Hester Prynne in *The Scarlet Letter* (1850), how to live between these extremities of the self, between the red man's wilderness and the white man's Boston.

In the eighth and longest sketch of "The Encantadas," included in *The Piazza Tales* (1856), Herman Melville depicts Hunilla as a Peruvian half-blood woman living on an island with her husband of pure Castilian blood and her brother of pure Indian blood. Hunilla's dual heritage emblemizes, for Melville, the diametrical opposites of life, the dark and light sides of existence explored in many of his works and particularly in *The Piazza Tales*, in which the irresolvable tension generated by the antagonistic forces of the unconscious and the conscious mind, of the irrational and the rational self, of freedom and fate, of the New and the Old World, among others, is carefully dramatized. The enigma of such conflict in the nature of creation is objectified in the terrain of the Galápagos Islands, a locale paradoxically suggesting the end as well as the beginning of time; in the indigenous tortoises, revealing a dark upperside and a light underside; and in the pirate visitors, evincing traces of goodness beneath a demonstrable depravity. This fundamental split in nature (at least as man experiences nature) and in humanity is symbolized by Hunilla's dual heritage; and the Christ imagery associated with her in the sketch not only emphasizes the junction of disparate extremes in her (for Christ joined the divine and the mundane) but also suggests her crucifixion, as it were, upon these antagonistic forces.

Hunilla's story appropriately appears between an account of Charles Isle (the seventh sketch), in which a Creole ignorantly tries to impose order upon chaos, and an account of Hood's Isle (the ninth sketch), in which Oberlus, "a European bringing into this savage region qualities more diabolical than are to be found among any of the surrounding cannibals,"[47] delights in anarchistic cruelty. Hunilla's story, then, appears between the Creole's attempt at civilization and Oberlus's manifestation of barbarism, for her divided self evinces a civilized regard for community as well as an Indian's relish for stoical solitariness. The sailors, who rescue her long after the death of her husband and brother, admire her as Christlike not because of any redemptive promise in her suffering but simply because in her experience of "a Spanish and an Indian grief," in her example of "a heart of yearning [civilized sense of community] in a frame of steel [savage sense of stoical solitude]," [48] they perceive the light and dark sides of life, the humane and savage, the divine and the diabolical—a contrast epitomizing humanity's martyrdom on the cross of life's numerous and irresolvable dichotomies. Like Hawthorne, Melville, at least at this late time of his career, suggests that everyone is, in a sense, a half-blood living in a world of apparently inexplicable bifurcation while trying to integrate a divided self; and the result of both endeavors is the painful, unredemptive crucifixion of Christlike humanity by and upon the conflicting forces of existence.

Melville, then, makes excellent symbolic use of his half-blood protagonist, but the metaphysical weight she is made to bear separates her from immediate involvement in the cultural context we have been describing; as a Peruvian living somewhere among the Galápagos Islands, she is far removed from the specific questions about America's destiny that normally inform, in one way or another, fictional treatments of the half-blood. A regional contemporary, John Neal, demonstrates less artistic talent than Melville, but he explores the symbolic possibilities of the half-blood, particularly as related to America, more fully than any other eastern author of the period.

In *Rachel Dyer* (1828), perhaps his best novel, [49] Neal depicts the conflict between the artificial power of established authority and the more elemental power of the independent self. The former is expressed in the static laws of an Old World civilization emphasizing conformity to external prohibitive social norms; the latter is expressed in the antinomian impulse of a New World experience emphasizing a self-reliant harkening to permissive and asocial internal values. Neal dramatizes this antagonism by means of symbolic detail and characterization, particularly in the portrait of his half-blood protagonist, implying that this tension results in a revolutionary impulse identifying the true American, providing the basis for a newly emerging American society, and distinguishing genuine American art.

Of the images which Neal manages consistently in his depiction of the conflict between authority and the self, the most prominent derive from the archetypal contest between light and dark. These images do not merely establish emotional atmosphere but define, in a conventional and rudimentary manner, the two coordinates of the thematic center of the novel. Imagery pertaining to light identifies the force of social authority, whereas that pertaining to darkness relates to the puissance of the self. Light illuminates external reality, and throughout *Rachel Dyer* Neal impugns Puritan Salem society, particularly as reflected in its legal system, for focusing exclusively on circumstantial and superficial evidence. At George Burroughs's trial the magistrates call for the lighting of torches in order to counter the sudden encroachment of darkness, the darkness of the mysterious, frightening, asocial energies of the self evident in Burroughs.

Burroughs, however, does not function as Neal's antithesis to Salem society. Opposed to the "illuminating" force of civilization is the Indian, "the *dark* Savage" inhabiting the "*shadow*" of the great western wilderness"[50] (my emphasis). The "wild men" dwelling in the "great shadowy woods" (pp. 22, 152) evince the anarchistic instinct of the self at war (literally in the novel) with the repressive voice of social authority arising from Salem's clearing in the wilderness. For Neal, "the barbarians and the savages" value life most because they represent the self's internal dark impulse which is essential to life but which the Old World civilization seeks to annihilate, the same shadowy force suggested by Neal's seemingly offhanded observations that witches never perform their mischief in the light of day and that Abigail Paris became increasingly darker in complexion the more she experienced the effects of witchcraft (pp. 104, 136, 196).

Both white (civilization) and dark (wilderness), Burroughs is a half-blood symbolizing Neal's notion of the true American. Burroughs's affinity for civilization is most apparent in those periods of his life when he "traversed the whole of Europe" and when he served as a Joshua to the residents of Casco Bay, a village under siege by Indians (pp. 153–54). More often, for reasons dictated by the plot of *Rachel Dyer*, Neal stresses the darker features of his swarthy protagonist, who not only grew up in the midst of savage warfare but can with ease assume the identity of an Indian (pp. 149–50, 168). This feature of Burroughs is highlighted by several conventional Gothic devices, such as his introduction in the novel as "a stranger . . . in the shadow of the huge trees that over-hung the doorway like a summer cloud," his possession of a "great black stallion," his defiance of "the Power of Darkness" before which others tremble, and his arrival at Paris's home in "pitchdark" (pp. 68, 88, 144, 174).

Accenting his ironic use of light imagery in reference to authority and contributing to his depiction of Burroughs as a representative of both civilization and the wilderness, is Neal's attribution to his protagonist of an inner fire. Because of its mysterious nature, the Salem citizens interpret this fire as darkness, but for Neal it is the real foundation of society. Seemingly conventional references to Burroughs's "bright fierce look," to the "fire flash[ing] from his eyes," and his manner of probing a problem "as with fire" (pp. 68, 72, 174) emphasize his possession of an interior illumination. This feature of the self is related to the "light" of social authority, a point intimated in Burroughs's assertion to the court, "my feet are upon the foundations of your strength" (p. 241). Compared to Burroughs's inner fire inflaming the wild power of the self, the flickering torchlight of authority proves artificial and weak. Those living in the wan illumination of authority, reflecting the once familiar and now abandoned "fire-sides of Europe" (p. 22), respond to hints of the genuine source of this light "with unspeakable terror," interpret them as expressions of a demonic "dark" power, and so reduce Burroughs to the status of "an outcast and fugitive, pursued by the law" (pp. 82, 178).

As a half-blood combining the instinct of the red race and the ethics of the white race, however, Burroughs never polarizes his identity. Exemplifying Neal's conception of a true American, Burroughs does not choose one side over the other. In his younger years he wrestled with the decision of whether he should pursue "further into the cities of Europe, or go back into the wilderness of America" (p. 104). But an older Burroughs fully embraces his double heritage in spite of the fact that at times he is ashamed of his relationship to civilization and that Neal uses him generally

as a foil for social authority: "As a white man, I will not war with
white men. As the adopted of the red men . . . with the blood of
a red man boiling in my heart, as the captive and nursling of the
brave Iroquois, I will not be the foe of a red man" (p. 171; author's ellipsis). Because the Indians fear his whiteness and the colonists fear his savage inner power—Burroughs is "a creature of tre-
mendous power" in body, mind, and words (pp. 222, 225, 237)
disporportionate to his external anatomical appearance[51]—he has
learned to accept his twilight existence between the warring forces
symbolized by the wilderness and civilization.

Elizabeth and Rachel Dyer likewise lead a twilight existence,
literally "living on the outskirts of the wood" (p. 203) between the
Indians and the colonists. Rachel, rather than Elizabeth, represents
the feminine equivalent to Burroughs. When Neal indicates that
she stood "in the dark part of the [meeting] house" where "the
shadow of a mighty tree fell so as to darken all the faces about
her" (pp. 129, 147), he introduces her in a manner very similar
to the initial appearance of Burroughs. Like Burroughs, moreover,
Rachel not only lives between the wilderness and civilization but
readily interacts with both red and white races (p. 200). Likewise,
the Dyers "belong to neither side in the war" between the Indians
and the Salem residents (p. 205). And Rachel's red hair, freed from
the symbolic confines of her cap and "shining . . . with a frightful
fixed gleam" (p. 226), corresponds to Burroughs's terrifying fiery
looks. A pariah, Rachel is said to lead a charmed life rather like
that of Burroughs, who is thought to be insane (pp. 88, 206).
Their alienated relation to established society is an intensified version of Mary Conant's and Charles Brown's rebellious disposition
toward Puritan society in *Hobomok*.

By introducing the detail that Rachel is a Quaker,[52] Neal forges
another link between his two protagonists and broadens their symbolic function. As a Quaker, Rachel is an outcast in Salem (a
community of Congregationalists) and, without totally repudiating
civilization, she relies on an inspiring Inner Light, on the "inward
prompting" of the shadowy power of the self so feared by the Salem
witch-hunters. Rachel's Quaker faith in the Inner Light corresponds
to Burroughs's trust in the antinomian impulse of the independent
self, in spite of the fact that nominally he is a Congregationalist
minister. At one point Burroughs concludes that he is "a messenger

of the Most High"; he believes "the dead of the night," when one's thoughts turn inward, is the time when God, "the Searcher of Hearts," speaks most effectively (p. 173). When he asserts that his feet stand upon the foundation of the magistrates' strength, Burroughs declares that what the judges do by the power of their authority—"which is, to deal with the creatures of God, as God himself professes to deal with them" (p. 102)—he can similarly perform by the more elemental power of a divinely inspired interior light which is in fact the very source of external legal authority. Like a Quaker, Burroughs believes he speaks "by authority of *one* who hath endowed me with great power" (p. 223).

Neal prepares the reader for this emphasis on Rachel and George's mutual trust in the interior power of the self by referring early in the novel to Elizabeth Hutchinson (he means Ann, of course). As a critic recently remarked, "Virtually all commentators have recognized that in New England, in dialectic with the Puritan Way, Ann Hutchinson and the Quakers go together; that the latter represent, chiefly a more organized and self-consciously sectarian espousal of the values of individualistic (or 'spiritual') freedom which is the essence of Ann Hutchinson's doctrine." [53] Emphasizing that Hutchinson was "one of the most extraordinary women of the age," that she was a close friend of Rachel's mother, and that she spoke with "awful power" about a "new faith" as if she had "authority from above" (pp. 36–41), [54] Neal carefully associates antinomianism and Quakerism. The Salem residents believe that their trouble with the Indians signifies the actualization of Hutchinson's fearful prophecy, and they are correct: the Indians represent the dark power of the antinomian self that has once again returned to confront (through racial warfare) and to haunt (through witchcraft performed only at night) the force of authority, which denies its relation to the more fundamental savage power of man's interior and thereby makes fugitives and sacrificial victims of such people as the Dyers and Burroughs. Unlike George and Rachel, the Salem community, those Old World emigrants who fearfully left behind their reassuring fireside society, cannot cope with the inner power of the self symbolized and stimulated into expression by the "shadow of the great western wilderness." Unable to reconcile the "dark savage" power of the self and Old World authority, Salem goes insane, undertakes the crazed persecution of anyone who seems to evince the witchery or dark powers of the self, and steadily destroys itself.

In *Rachel Dyer* Neal celebrates the promise of a fresh society, one indigenous to the New World reconciling self and community, a society of half-bloods, as it were. Sharing a faith in the self and experiencing similar circumstances, George and Rachel adumbrate a new alternative society. At the conclusion of the novel Rachel kisses George, an act suggestive of their own sense of family or social cohesion. They cannot marry—Neal's symbol for the actualization of social identity[55]—because the new community they symbolize has not yet arisen. Their deaths will serve as a sacrifice (Neal's word) requisite for an emerging New World society in which Elizabeth Dyer, who is spared, "will have sympathy" (p. 260).

This new community will not annihilate but will accommodate the self. It will displace the life-destroying, wilderness-leveling fears of an Old World society antagonistic to the vital impulse of the self. It will, in Neal's opinion, supplant a Calvinistic life-negating belief in a transcendent God, emphasizing external legalisms, with a secular, life-engendering trust in a social authority derived from the self's manifestation of internal virtue. As Neal's prototype of the "half-breed" citizens of this new community, Burroughs readily departs from Congregationalist dogma, most significantly when he advises Rachel to prevaricate and confess her guilt so that she may live to "do much good on earth" (p. 257). No conscientious New England Puritan minister of 1692 would give this advice, least of all for the reasons Burroughs cites; for the Puritan, truth before God mattered above all else regardless of its consequences in the material world. Burroughs, however, responds to an inner authority and consequently advocates a variety of what is known today as "situation ethics,"[56] explaining to Rachel: "What I have said to you, I have been constrained to say, for it is a part of my faith Rachel, that as we believe, so are we judged: and that therefore, had you believed it to be right for you to confess and live, it would have been right, before the Lord" (p. 257). No orthodox Puritan could have espoused such a notion, one clearly stressing the primacy of the self's authority. Burroughs affirms action based on the inner self's sense of social ethics rather than on mere conformity to external authority and the fear of God.

Burroughs's concern over public welfare suggests that the free expression of the self in America will not result in anarchy but will somehow give rise to a new society which will prove less structured and more liberated than the Old World civilization, yet will impart broader social purpose to the energies of the self. Although *Rachel Dyer* ostensibly dramatizes the conflict in seventeenth-century America between the self and social authority, the central focus of the novel is on its two protagonists—one a literal and the other a figurative half-breed—as prototypical Americans transforming the antinomian impulse stimulated by the New World experience into a burgeoning social order deriving from and somehow accommodating the self. Without the metamorphosis provided by the American experience, the mysterious "dark" self would tend toward anarchistic savagery and would manifest the deformity the Old World attributes to it. Neal acknowledges the external deformities which the eruptions of the self are prone to produce—hence Burroughs's altered swarthy appearance and small stature and Rachel's unattractive freckled face and "distorted shape" resulting from her humped back (p. 226). But he also warns against assessing value and beauty by superficial evidence or externals illuminated by a light revealing merely surfaces: "We may be deceived, if we venture to judge of the inward by the outward man" (p. iii). Rachel and George evince an inward force resulting in certain unattractive and anarchistic deformities in the external concerns of the Old World society, but nonetheless proving potentially beautiful and valuable with regard to the internal virtue of an emerging New World community. As Neal explained in 1825: "We require of the American people, great power, stout, original power; productions, whatever else they may be, indigenous to the country; preferring those which are decidedly vicious, to those which are of a neutral character"; "give us that which is able to be mischievous, if unrighteously, or unworthily administered" because "whatever is incapable of doing mischief, is incapable of doing good."[57] In his literal and figurative half-blood protagonists, Neal portrays the shadowy power of the self as an apparent deformity (dark and savage) which in actuality provides the basis (an inner light) for the evolution of New World social ethics organic to the self.

In the completed novel as well as in the earlier, shorter version of *Rachel Dyer*, Neal intended to employ "the language of immortal, indistructable spirits" in order to create "a portrait of man—a history of the human heart" (p. ix). By delving into the "dark" force of the self in reaction to confining social authority, as centralized in the half-blood natures of George and Rachel, Neal explored the antinomian inward promptings shared by all humans but especially evident as the power infusing an emerging American civilization and literature. In Neal's view American literature reflects an evolving New World society derived from, accommodating, and containing without stifling the inward prompting of self stimulated into expression by contact with the free, life-loving "dark savage" dwelling in the shadowy wilderness (an externalization of the self's interior reality). *Rachel Dyer* celebrates a vision of America's fresh future society in a prose style which, in Neal's opinion,[58] is emancipated from Old World authority. Not rigid like the external legalism of Old World established authority or chaotic like the internal elemental power of the self's anarchistic impulse, the prose in this novel was designed by Neal to convey, as it were, a half-blood style mirroring the integration of antinomian impulse (the self's power) and social ethics (community's accommodating authority) in his literal and figurative half-blood protagonists, an ideal integration informing Neal's vision of a looming new American society (half civilized, half wild) and of its burgeoning indigenous literature.

Whatever the overall deficiencies of his novel, Neal's fictional management of the half-blood, compared to that of his contemporaries, emerges as the most complexly developed and the most fully realized portrait. What Neal's depiction of Burroughs lacks in genuine flesh and blood, in contrast to half-bloods in nineteenth-century nonfiction narratives, it gains in symbolic richness. Like Melville, Neal scrutinized the universal implications of the mixed-blood Indian; but he emphasized the uniquely American features of the half-blood and, unlike most other eastern writers of the nineteenth century, successfully translated this emphasis into an unsubverted, artistically controlled aesthetic vision of America. Moreover, in presenting Rachel Dyer as a figurative half-blood, Neal anticipated another pattern in contemporary fictional treatments of the mixed-blood Indian: the substitution of half-bloods in spirit for half-bloods in fact, the subject of the next chapter.

4

Merely Yokoto Stain ∾

Several of John Neal's contemporary eastern novelists apparently felt more comfortable substituting the figurative half-blood, a half-blood in spirit or temperament, for the literal mixed-blood Indian.[1] This strategy permitted writers to escape an often artistically fatal conflict which tended to emerge in works treating half-bloods, because it afforded them the best of two worlds. Unlike the literal mixed-blood Indian—the dubious spawn of miscegenation and the uncertain amalgamation of the best and worst features of his dual heritage—the figurative half-blood was a pure white who evinced the virtues of both the noble savage and civilization; frequently he was compared to, or thought to be, or described as if he were an actual half-blood. The half-blood in spirit represented a compromise that permitted authors to make artistic use of this new phenomenon, particularly as a symbol of America's difference from Europe, without having to wrestle with an irrational fear, in themselves or in society, of miscegenation, or with the half-blood's implicit perpetuation of savagery, which, however latent, might later erupt or undermine civilization.

This strategy is suggested in *A Tour on the Prairies*, in which (as we saw in the first chapter) Washington Irving struggles with his ambivalence toward Pierre Beatte and recommends for youth a "previous tour" on the frontier, thereby in effect indicating that civilization would benefit not from literal half-bloods but from, as it were, youthful figurative half-bloods who acquire from a *brief* experience with the prairies only the beneficial attributes of Beatte. In a more limited sense this division between literal and figurative half-bloods appears in *Recollections of the Last Ten Years in the Valley of the Mississippi*, in which (as we also remarked in the first chapter) Timothy Flint recoils at the idea of intermarriage between the red and white races but, at one point, evades this reality of the half-bloods in order to advance the idealistic possibility that they might

provide a link between civilization and barbarism, a link theoretically facilitating the Christianization of the Indian.

Undoubtedly the prototypical half-blood in spirit is Natty
Bumppo, the protagonist in James Fenimore Cooper's *Leatherstock-
ing Tales*. Natty emanates from Cooper's desire to create a heroic
white figure who adheres to certain essential civilized values and
at the same time acquires certain virtuous attributes of the noble
savage. Cooper's attitude toward literal half-bloods appears in *The
Prairie* (1827), in which Natty thinks, "The half-and-halfs that one
meets in these distant districts are altogether more barbarous than
the real savage." In a footnote to this remark, Cooper observes:
"Half-breeds; men born of Indian women by white fathers. This race
has much of the depravity of civilization without the virtues of the
savage."[2] Underlying Cooper's view *may* be his fear of miscegenation, as some critics would have us believe,[3] but the apparent
source, reflecting more ambivalence than alarm, is Cooper's firm
conviction that every race has a distinct integrity which is un-
naturally violated in cross-breeding. In *The Last of the Mohicans*
(1826), for instance, Natty's somewhat irritating refrain about his
freedom from any taint of Indian blood parallels Chingachgook's
equivalent pride in the fact that his own blood is pure. Cooper
sees the Indians in general as morally inferior to whites, but the
doctrine of racial gifts, which Natty time and again remarks, seems
to imply, as one critic has recently observed, "a separate but at
least equal relationship between the two races."[4]

Even Cooper's management of raven-haired Cora Munro, whose
West Indian mother was remotely descended from a black slave,
suggests his repudiation of literal cross-breeding and, at the same
time, his fascination with *the idea* of interracial hybrids. It is Major
Heyward, not Cooper, who reacts to Cora with a prejudice "as
deeply rooted as if it had been ingrafted in his nature" and who,
as a southerner, later confesses, "To me her worth was in a degree
obscured" (2:188, 313). The novel itself evinces a counter-current;
for Cora's and Uncas's mutual love provides intrinsic romantic
interest, a feature intensified by the ceremony held during Cora's
funeral. During the ceremony, Indian maidens sing of Cora's "blood
purer and richer than the rest of her nation" (2:415), and they
proclaim an eternal marriage between Cora and Uncas in the spiri-

tual world. Reflecting on "the error of their simple creed," Natty shakes his head (2:416). Natty does not refute the idea of life after death but rather the notion that after death the "gifts" or talents defining the integrity of a race and distinguishing it from another will disappear; this is why he again shakes his head when Munro speaks of heaven as a place where all races will assemble "without distinction of sex, or rank, or color" (2:420).

These two conflicting currents can again be seen in Cooper's *The Wept of Wish-Ton-Wish* (1829), in which miscegenation occurs and a half-blood child is born. In this novel the daughter of Content and Ruth Heathcote, a blue-eyed blond also named Ruth, marries Conanchet, an Indian, and bears a child. The half-blood child evinces "physical excellence" and occasions "maternal joy" in his grandmother; even his grandfather grudgingly accepts him, rationalizing that it is God's "will that one sprung of heathen lineage shall come beneath my roof" (22:357, 358, 368). A peripheral but telling dialogue concerning the child occurs in the novel when the child's mother argues that cross-breeding between the red and white races is good, even as the European apple was grafted "on the thorn of our woods, and the fruit is good" (22:396). Her Indian spouse, however, believes it to be bad that their child is "neither red nor pale," but neither he nor Cooper answers Ruth's question whether her son is a good "fruit"; so the dialogue is never completed. Conanchet dies, soon followed by his wife, who expires during a fit of mental derangement. We never learn of the fate of their half-blood son, who presumably continues to live with his white grandparents. Even if, like *The Last of the Mohicans*, it seems to suggest the unnaturalness of miscegenation between races, *The Wept of Wish-Ton-Wish* curiously raises more questions about the subject than it answers. Like Conanchet, it avoids a direct reply on the issue of miscegenation.

Cooper's simultaneous negative sentiment and artistic fascination with this subject crystalize in his portrait of Natty Bumppo. As a "link between them [the Indians] and civilized life," as "one whose skin is neither red nor pale" (2:421, 350), Natty epitomizes the strategy of some eastern writers to create half-bloods in spirit in order to avoid the problems contingent on portraits of literal half-bloods (summarized, perhaps, in Ruth's unanswered question in *The Wept of Wish-Ton-Wish*) and at the same time to realize certain artistic benefits latent in the frontier hybrid race. In contrast to the actual half-bloods defamed in *The Prairie*, Natty combines only the best features of both races. When, for instance, he is about to slay Magua, who has tried to force Cora into cohabitation with him, Natty hesitates (as Gordon did in "The Bois Brulé") because he "believed such an act, however congenial it might be to the nature of an Indian, utterly unworthy of one who boasted a descent from men that knew no cross of blood" (2:321). Even though Natty must die before the sweep of civilization (in *The Prairie*), like so many literal half-bloods of nineteenth-century fiction, he only figuratively combines white ethics and red virtues. As a half-blood in spirit, rather than in fact, Natty represents an idealistic embodiment of the frontier hybrid race; Cooper, then, could at once feel comfortable with him and attribute symbolic value to him. In figurative half-bloods like Natty, eastern writers moved beyond a personal or social ambivalence, which tended to subvert authorial designs, and from a safe distance explored the artistic possibilities of the half-blood.

There were countless imitations of Natty Bumppo—fictional trappers, frontiersmen, mountainmen, or "white savages" to some degree modelled after Daniel Boone. Richard Slotkin has detailed the variations, often regionally determined, of the Boone figure mediating between symbolic savagery and society, reconciling a democratic-barbaric wilderness and a stratified refined civilization.[5] Few of these Boone figures, however, were as implicitly identified with the half-blood as is Cooper's protagonist, even when they replaced the mixed-blood by embodying something of his symbolic potentiality; this is true of Ipsico Poe, who in Bird's *A Belated Revenge* adopts frontiersman Nelson as a surrogate father after Poe's experiences with Craven, an Indian-souled white man. Rarely did the Boone figure per se require idiosyncratic literary strategies of the sort evident so often in nineteenth-century fiction treating half-bloods.

The type of substitution directly pertinent to the concerns of our discussion appears blatantly in the first Beadle Dime Novel, *Malaeska* (1839, 1860) by Ann S. Stephens, a New Englander who edited such periodicals as the *Portland Magazine* and the New York City-based *Ladies Companion*. Stephens's novel concerns the secret marriage of a white man to an Indian maiden and the birth of a mixed-blood child named William Danforth. William's dual heritage disturbs his father, who at an insensitive moment says to his wife, "It's a pity the little fellow is not quite white."[6] The remark grieves Malaeska, his wife; but her husband has been emotionally plagued by his marriage to her, and whenever he debates with himself whether to reveal his family to his own parents, "his affections struggle powerfully with his pride" as he envisions "his disgrace" and "the scorn with which his parents and sisters would receive the Indian wife and half-Indian child" (p. 40). After Danforth's death, his father indeed reacts with disgust when the marriage is disclosed, forcibly separating the child from his mother and sending him to Europe so that his heritage may be refined. William's grandfather "gladly would . . . have rent the two races asunder, in the very person of his grandchild, could the pure half of his being been thus preserved" (p. 84).

The novel, however, does not repudiate William's Indian heritage so directly. It also emphasizes Malaeska's "untutored heart, rich in . . . natural affections," and her manifestation of "all that was strong, picturesque, and imaginative in savage life, with the delicacy, sweetness, and refinement which follows in the train of civilization" (pp. 31, 158–59). Malaeska's virtues are not to be ignored, and Stephens introduces Sarah Jones, a white child who attaches herself to Malaeska and especially admires the Indian maiden's "refinement of principle and feeling" (p. 160). With the single exception of Malaeska, who "is white in education, feeling, every thing but color" (p. 222), Sarah claims to have no affection for the red race.

William eventually returns from Europe. Culturally refined and an intense Indian hater (the result of his grandfather's sentiment and of his father's murder by Indians), William falls in love with Sarah, and, both ignorant of his mixed blood, they become engaged. Just as it appears that Malaeska's real son and her, as it were, adopted daughter are about to marry, William makes the startling discovery that his mother is an Indian and that he is a half-blood. Bewileredly he utters, "I was about to be married to one so gentle— so pure—I, an Indian—was about to give my stained hand to a lovely being of untainted blood" (p. 243). Unable to live with his newly revealed dual identity, he commits suicide and is soon followed by his Indian mother, "the heart-broken victim of an un-

natural marriage" (p. 253). The entire episode results in the destruction of the Danforth line, and in time all trace of the family
estate vanishes. Sarah, as sentimental tradition would have it, remains inconsolably saddened, but Stephens tells us, very vaguely,
that she led a useful life. As a figurative half-blood, as Malaeska's
adopted child evincing the best virtues of the white and red races,
Sarah emerges in the novel as the center of attention. In every
respect she makes a suitable mate for William, but, typically, William must die. Whatever uniquely American traits William, the
literal half-blood, might symbolize are transposed to Sarah, the half-
blood in spirit, who evinces the best features of both races without
possessing the actual "savage" blood which, it was feared, might
lie latent only to erupt eventually and shatter civilization.

Equally interesting instances of half-blood bifurcation and of the
half-blood in spirit occur in the work of Albert W. Aiken, another
easterner. Aiken's *The Indian Mazeppa* (1878) relates the story of
a brother and sister whose Indian mother and Mexican father are
murdered by Bandera, their father's brother, disguised as an Indian.
Removed for their safety, the children are soon separated and grow
to maturity unaware of each other and of their origin. In contrast
to Snelling and Jones, Aiken avoids treating his half-blood characters in this novel as divided individuals; he conveniently emphasizes only one side in each of them. Silver-Spear, young and beautiful, is a free spirit, but she clearly favors white ways, worships
the Christian deity, and always refers to herself as a Mexican; by
the end of the novel she marries Bandera's pure-blooded son, Luis,
and together they do very well. Juan, however, is in fact White
Mustang, a chief of the Comanches, who revengefully seeks the life
of his uncle and the hand of Bandera's white daughter, Giralda;
he tricks his uncle, appropriately, by disguising himself as a member
of civilization (thereby redressing his uncle's earlier deception in
Indian guise), and after capturing Bandera he says of himself, "The
chief is all Indian now."[7]

Aiken's ambivalence toward Juan and half-bloods in general derives less from their alleged cunning than from the apparent ease
with which they can mask their inner selves and readily slip into
or out of civilization at will, a feature emphasized in Aiken's *The
Fresh on the Rio Grande* (1887) and *Dick Talbot, the Ranch King*
(1892).[8] So, whereas Silver-Spear is portrayed in terms of the more

sympathetic treatment generally accorded half-blood women in real life and in fiction during the period, White Mustang is doomed to the fatal pattern so characteristic of fictional male half-bloods, a destiny particularly necessitated by his function as the repository of the Indian side of both himself and his sister. In a surprising final chapter, White Mustang is suddenly strangled to death by the Madman of the Plains, in actuality his father, who had been presumed dead but who in fact had survived his brother's attack, although he is now bereft of reason—a character reminiscent of Frampton in Simms's two novels. By killing his son, the repository of the Indian features of his children, Juan's father saves Giralda from a coerced mixed marriage, guarantees Silver-Spear the inheritance of his estate, and (we might add) atones for having married an Indian—an atonement epitomized by his demented suicidal leap from a cliff immediately after the murder of his son. As the embodiment of the Indian side of his own and his sister's dual heritage, Juan dies so that Silver-Spear, the embodiment of the white-civilized side of their divided nature, can inherit the estate and marry Luis. Juan's perverse attempt to force Giralda into marriage and subsequently into primitive ways is supplanted by Silver-Spear's marriage to Luis, an act (like the death of her brother) consummating the demise of her red heritage and the victory of white values in herself (already disposed toward civilization) and on her Texas estate on the frontier (a half-savage region slowly but steadily being domesticated).

The balance achieved in *The Indian Mazeppa* vanishes in Aiken's badly managed *Talbot in Apache Land* (1892), another novel portraying two half-bloods. Chico Colorado, the daughter of an Indian chief and a Spanish captive, excels in mental gifts, appears "a very princess among her red sisters," and seems "a very Cleopatra in her wild, savage beauty."[9] But, Aiken cautions, she behaved "as though she had not a single drop of white blood in her veins" and, according to the novel's protagonist (Dick Talbot), "she is more like a wild beast than a human." Her beauty suggests the savage tiger: "Hid by the velvet paws were sharp nails which could rend or tear" (pp. 11, 19). In contrast is Annis Kruger, a half-blood woman who throughout the novel remains disguised as a young man named Alva. Aiken describes Alva, clearly hinting at "his" real identity as a woman (to be revealed later in the work), about seventeen or eighteen years old, below the medium height, but well-formed and muscular; his face was dark, rather inclined to be womanish, although there were strong lines about the mouth, and the firm-set chin seemed to show a resolute will. He was apparently a half-breed, for no other race than the wild Indian could have given him such a pair of black eyes. [p. 2]

Annis and Chico are rivals contesting for Dick Talbot, and their portraits are initially polarized, respectively, to the white and the red side of their mutually divided nature, just as were those of Silver-Spear and White Mustang in *The Indian Mazeppa*. But in the later novel Aiken loses control, a problem evident at every point in the work, and he permits his ambivalence free rein, with curious results.

For instance, Annis's representation of the Caucasoid side of her dual heritage exerts its own force when, carelessly but revealingly, Aiken refers to her as "the white girl" and has Chico call her "this white man-squaw" (pp. 14, 17), as if the author occasionally forgets she is a half-blood. The opposite feature of Aiken's ambivalence, however, counters this development. Aiken's dubiety in treating Annis as a heroine surfaces in his remarks about her lack of femininity, about how her half-blood wilderness life "partially unsexed" her and how "she could be depended upon to act with all a man's energy" (p. 14). "Remarkably muscular" and possessing an "iron will" (pp. 13, 20), Annis is no conventional nineteenth-century fictional heroine; as her half-blood racial status and her continual disguise as a man suggest, she is a misfit, albeit by no means a hideous one. The relation between Annis's "maleness" and Aiken's ambivalence becomes most pronounced when Annis uses her abnormal strength to overpower Chico (who has been compared to a tiger) and escapes captivity by disguising herself as her half-blood rival, a scene once again suggesting Aiken's unconscious anxiety over the ease with which the mixed-blood can readily enter or depart from civilization. Aiken's doubts overwhelm the latter half of his novel as Annis's Indian nature—the "disguised" Chico in her, now emergent after the assumption of Chico's identity—subversively asserts its dominance supplanting Aiken's earlier attempt to depict Annis in terms of white values. Late in the novel, for instance, Annis admits that perhaps she should be merciful to

Chico, who has shot Annis's father; but, Annis confesses, the murder "has made me fully as savage as any red-skin in the land, and I fairly hunger for revenge" (p. 20). Annis succeeds in killing Chico during an Indian raid, but she too is mortally wounded and dies as Dick kisses her for the first and last time. Aiken's ambivalence ceases only with the demise of both half-bloods, resolving the tension evident in his initial attempt to separate them.

Aiken's fascination with the dual nature of the half-blood also emerges in his portrait of the novel's protagonist. Dick Talbot, who has spent many years among the Indians in the wilderness, seems a good match for Annis. In fact not only are Dick's pants "a cross between the fringed leggings of the red skin and a pair of tightly-cut pantaloons," but his face is "very dark in hue, as though he had been exposed to the elements, or, possibly, he had Indian blood in his veins" (p. 2). But whereas half-blood Annis, after assuming Chico's identity, becomes increasingly "savage" in her obsession for revenge, Dick, who is not in fact a half-blood, becomes steadily more refined. In contrast to Annis's renunciation of Christian mercy, Dick finds himself, to his surprise, "getting so [he] hate[s] to shed blood unless it is impossible to avoid it" (p. 23) —a change rather similar to that of Gordon in Snelling's story.

A Mexican captive provides a direct counterpart to Dick's portrait and alerts us to the authorial uncertainty underlying that portrait. The Mexican is a "white Indian," an all-white man who disguises himself as an Indian and participates in Indian raids, so that his "hands are red . . . with the blood of [his] own race" (p. 23). Aiken senses, then, that literal half-bloods tend toward the primitive side of their heritage and that figurative half-bloods, like Dick, tend toward the "white savage." Aiken wishes to have Dick benefit from a vague half-blood context for his identity, but he fails to manage the matter and finally polarizes Dick toward the ethics of white civilization. Aiken may give his protagonist the nickname "Injun Dick" (in *Dick Talbot in No Man's Camp* [1892] and *Dick Talbot's Clean-Out* [1892]), but Talbot has brown hair (in *Talbot in Apache Land*) and gray-blue eyes (in *Dick Talbot's Close Call* [1893]). The expression "Injun Dick" refers to the fact that Talbot has lived among Indians, that he can survive in both red and white realms even though he is not an actual mixed-blood. Dick is a half-blood in spirit; he comes as close to being a half-blood as an all-white frontier character can, even looking as if he *possibly* has Indian blood in his veins, but he remains in fact, like Natty Bumppo, a man free from the cross of mixed blood.

Just as southern attitudes influenced southwestern fictional portraits of the half-blood, eastern attitudes affected midwestern accounts, as Snelling's "The Bois Brulé" demonstrates. Even in the West, eastern attitudes toward the mixed-blood Indian surfaced, particularly the literary strategy of substituting a half-blood in spirit for his literal counterpart. The work of Bret Harte, who in 1854 moved from New York to California (where he wrote his best stories and became a leader of literary activities until he left in 1871), is illustrative.

Harte's view of mixed-blood Indians remains uncertain, but it seems to approach Alexander Ross's in equity. On the one hand, Harte mentions their deficiencies. In "The Argonauts of North Liberty" (1877), Cherokee Bob, a blackmailer who runs a gang of road agents, is referred to as a "mongrel half-breed."[10] A character in this story remarks, "the men are Mexican half-breeds just as Bob's a half Cherokee. The sooner that kind o' cross cattle exterminate each other the better it'll be for the country" (11:225). In "The Mermaid of Lighthouse Point" (1903) a half-blood woman is sold for fifty dollars; in "Snow-Bound at Eagle's" (1885) a wretched Mexican half-blood steals from his master and is trapped in snow; and in "The Princess Bob and Her Friends" (1870) an Indian woman remains immune to civilized influences, bears a half-blood child, and dies trying to locate the white husband who has deserted her. On the other hand, "A Pupil of Chestnut Ridge" (1903) dramatizes the plight of a half-blood girl as a result of "the strong racial antagonism toward the negro and Indian by . . . Southwestern" settlers. And "In the Carquinez Woods" (1883) presents the story of Low Dorman, a kind-hearted half-blood botanist, whose mixed blood repels Nellie Wynn, a representative of white society; he appeals to Teresa, a tough, socially-ostracized dancing girl of Spanish descent, who thinks, "I reckon he's neither worse nor better" for being a half-blood "and perhaps he wasn't as particular in his tastes as a white man might have been" about her (4:95).

These portraits reflect Harte's tendency, like Ross's and Chopin's, to see the half-blood as an outcast in white society and as a human being subject to the gamut of life's vices and virtues. Harte's most extensive comments about the mixed-blood Indian occur in "The Ancestors of Peter Atherly" (1897). Atherly, the son of a white mother and an Indian father, is a congressman who risks the disdain of his California constituency by advocating Indian rights. Beleaguered by an uncertainty as to which race deserves his loyalty, he undergoes an identity crisis, which is aggravated by his twin sister's manifestation of strange fits of excitement emanating from the uncontrollable latent Indian or "savage" side of her nature. (Harte's strategy of bifurcation recalls Aiken's earlier *The Indian Mazeppa*.) Intensifying Atherly's problem is his affection for Lady Elfrida Runnybroke, an Englishwoman of society who loathes Indians and asserts that "mixed races never attain to anything" (16:51). Atherly formulates his response to her in writing:

I am satisfied that much of the mischievous and extravagant prejudice against the half-breed and all alliances of the white and red races springs from the ignorance of the frontiersman and his hasty generalization of facts. There is no doubt that an intermixture of blood brings out purely superficial contrasts the more strongly, and that against the civilizing habits and even çostumes of the half-breed, certain Indian defects appear the more strongly as in the case of the color line of the quadroon and octoroon, but it must not be forgotten that these are only the contrasts of specific improvement, and the inference that the borrowed defects of the full-blooded aborigine is utterly illogical.

Through Atherly, Harte (who was partly Jewish[11]) refutes the notion of the mixed-blood Indian as half red, half white, and half devil; he indicates that the half-blood is necessarily neither an improvement nor a perversion, that he is no worse than either side of his heritage. Atherly's defensive posture, however, seems to define the limits of Harte's view, which falls short of asserting any superior features in the half-blood; and indeed Harte's noble spokesman dies with his sister in order to save Lady Elfrida. Paralleling the demise of Eumea in Rowson's novel as well as of George Burroughs and Rachel Dyer in Neal's novel, the Atherlys' death is presented as sacrificial. Nevertheless, the death represents a typical outcome for fictional half-bloods; its sacrificial nature ennobles the mixed-blood character while at the same time it removes the fundamental problems his identity presents to the writer.

Harte's evasion of the central issues involved in this matter can better be appreciated by remarking how his treatment of Jack Hamlin changes, how Hamlin is transformed from an actual to a figurative half-blood. Hamlin appears in twenty of Harte's works, the largest number of appearances of any Harte character save Colonel Starbottle, who also is present in twenty stories. Hamlin is introduced in "Brown of Calaveras" (1870), in which he is referred to as Camanche Jack. A professional gambler, Jack exhibits, to the advantage of his vocation, "an Indian stoicism—said to be an inheritance from his maternal ancestor" (1:66). Several characteristics ascribed to Hamlin in this story remain unchanged in his appearances in later stories: his loyalty to friends, his detached attitude toward women, his skepticism, his gravity, his "self-contained air," and his role as a "lonely calculator of chances" (1:65). His language and manners, however, do become increasingly refined, his handsomeness is more emphasized, and his half-blood nature is eventually forgotten.

The moderate refinement of Hamlin's language and manners can be seen in a comparison of "The Iliad of Sandy Bar," "How Santa Claus Came to Simpson's Bar," "The Fool of Five Forks," "An Heiress of Red Dog" and "A Passage in the Life of Mr. John Oakhurst," all of which first appeared between 1870 and 1875, with "An Apostle of the Tules," "A Knight Errant of the Foot-Hills," "A Sappho of Green Springs," "A First Family of Tasajara," "The Bell-Ringer of Angel's," "A Protegée of Jack Hamlin's," "Three Partners" (especially this story), and "Mr. Jack Hamlin's Mediation," all of which appeared between 1883 and 1899. In these later stories, Hamlin's language becomes more grammatical and less vernacular, his manners more refined, his tastes more fastidious, and his features more handsome. His fondness for children is introduced and his eye color is changed from "wicked black" (2:289) to brown with "a certain dancing devilry" in it (15:15).

It is interesting to note, I think, that Hamlin's metamorphosis occurs after the appearance of Harte's novel *Gabriel Conroy* (1876). This fairly complex, somewhat tedious story concerns complications engendered by mistaken and assumed identities; but, for our purposes, the experience of Doña Dolores Salvatierra, who is really Grace Conroy, is most important. According to rumor, Dolores's mother is an Indian; and, as another character explains, "she might have had a pretty complexion, for some of these half-breeds are nearly white, but she had been stained when an infant with some barbarous and indelible dye, after the savage custom of her race" (13:151).[12] Suffering from "prejudices with which the old families have regarded her race and color" (13:152), Dolores lives in nun-like seclusion.

Jack Hamlin, who is not specifically referred to in the novel as a half-blood, feels that Dolores's "strange complexion" evinces "a bewildering charm" (13:230), a hint at the affinity he senses (apparently unconsciously) between their mutual half-blood natures. Whatever the reason, he is very attracted to her and when, on one occasion, she is spoken of as "that colored woman" (13: 80), he becomes enraged. In helping to resolve the plot of the novel, which focuses on the reinstatement of Gabriel Conroy to his inheritance and on the reunion (in marriage) of Grace (alias Dolores) and her early lover, Hamlin is fatally wounded. His death is as sacrificial as that of Atherly or of Burroughs, and it is followed by the demise, as it were, of the Indian half of Dolores. As a result of Hamlin's sacrifice Dolores's real identity as Grace Conroy is unveiled: "Wishing to keep her secret from the world and to prevent recognition by the members of her own race and family, by the assistance and advice of an Indian peon, Manuela, she consented that her face and hands should be daily washed by the juice of the Yokoto—whose effect is to change the skin to the color of bronze" (14:183). So the stain allegedly used on her by the Indians is not permanent, like the "stained hand" of Danforth in *Malaeska*; in fact, Grace is not a half-blood at all.[13]

Grace emerges as a version of the half-blood in spirit, exempt from the stain or taint of mixed blood but benefiting from identification with the half-blood. Her gains may be physical survival and material reward, whereas generally the half-blood in spirit profits more in virtue; but the strategy Harte employs is akin to that in Cooper's *The Last of the Mohicans*, Stephens's *Malaeska*, and Aiken's (later) *Talbot in Apache Land*. Significant, too, is the observation that Hamlin's death not only abolishes the Indian side of Dolores (Grace) but also the Indian side of Hamlin. It is not at all surprising to find one critic wondering whether Harte had by the end of the novel forgotten that Hamlin was a half-blood.[14] In his resurrection in the stories written after *Gabriel Conroy*, Hamlin's Indian heritage is, in fact, never mentioned; it is lost to the ascendancy of his white side—manifested in his refinement of language, manners, sentiment, and virtues—as if he too had been stained only temporarily. Hamlin, the literal half-blood, is reincarnated as Hamlin, the half-blood in spirit. Doubtless this mutation relates to Harte's decline as a writer after the early 1870s; but Hamlin's metamorphosis is nonetheless instructive. Harte's unwitting obliteration of Hamlin's Indian feature as if it were merely a temporary stain demonstrates an interesting variety of the eastern strategy of replacing the literal half-blood with the half-blood in spirit, while still artistically benefiting from the new American type provided by the mixed-blood Indian.

5

Frontier Robin Hood ∾

The half-blood, as we have seen, objectifies in his very being the conflict between the red and white races, and his portrayal in nineteenth-century American fiction emanates from uncertainty as to his malign or benign relation to white society and to its concern with New World promise.

In the fiction of the South, (e.g., Simms's *The Partisan*, Howard's *The Black Gauntlet*), he often stereotypically represents an evil force, a dubious, unnatural species engendered by abhorrent miscegenation and threatening the purity and the preservation of white civilization. This pattern reappears in the fiction of the Old and New Southwest (e.g., Steele's "The Scout's Mistake," Clemens's *The Adventures of Tom Sawyer*), but sometimes it is qualified by legend (as in Ransom's *Osceola*, Arrington's *The Rangers and Regulators of the Tanaha*, Ingraham's *The Phantom Mazeppa*) or by authorial concern with human psychology (Chopin's "Loka").

In the fiction of the East, Midwest and West, ambivalence toward the half-blood prevails, but this ambivalence permits a greater range of literary experimentation. Although the half-blood may still appear as a caricature in these works, he tends to be rendered more dramatically, either because of his inherent nature or because his nature contends with social or literary conventions. His potentiality for action is greater, his symbolic function generally more encompassing and controlled in the fiction of these regions. The quintessential question underlying these literary portraits of the mixed-blood Indian was: Does he represent a new, wonderful natural link between the red and white races symbolizing an emergent American identity or does he represent a degenerate, abnormal amalgamation of the worst vices of both races menacing the promise of a New World civilization? Half-blood characters seesaw on this question, the pivot being social and literary convention. In order to resolve the problem, such writers as Child, Snelling, Jones, and Aiken sometimes divided the half-blood, refining or eventually eliminating (often by sleight of hand) the Indian side of his nature. Others —Manning, Jackson, and Wheeler—reduced the function of the half-blood character, distanced themselves from him or her, or virtually ignored the implications of the mixed-blood's Indian side. Still others, such as Cooper, Stephens, Aiken, and Harte, substituted a half-blood in spirit for the half-blood in fact by creating a white character of untainted blood who achieved his identity from a half-blood-like existence and who spiritually or figuratively joined the virtues of the two races in his manner of life. This substitution was, so far as I can judge, never a fully conscious artistic strategy; it apparently emerged as a viable resolution, however tentative and ambiguous, maximizing the half-blood's symbolic possibilities while minimizing the social and literary conventions that generally impinged on portraits of literal half-bloods.

Half-bloods in spirit generally live, sometimes in sorrow, beyond the conclusion of the stories in which they appear. Their literal prototype, however, often dies, even as the noble savage expires time and again in the fiction of the century.[1] The half-blood dies because his life among frontier perils is precarious, because his genetic constitution is thought to be inferior, because his allegiance to the white race remains dubious, because his frontier proficiency and numerical dominance menace dependent and guilt-ridden white settlers, because, in short, his very being is enigmatically ambiguous. Killing off the half-blood is the simplest literary strategy for resolving the dilemma his existence poses; and his death usually results in something lost and something gained. Often in southern fiction his demise preserves the purity of white civilization. In eastern and western fiction his death is frequently elevated to a sacrifice allowing for a higher mode of society which the half-blood symbolically adumbrates; he or she dies so that Jeffy Oliver, Sarah Jones, Belle Bright, Lady Elfrida, Flora Cameron, Giralda Bandera, Dick Talbot, Grace Conroy, and Elizabeth Dyer may survive or remain untainted.

Although he shared the mulatto's tragic discontent resulting from an uncertain identity,[2] the half-blood appears to have been a "safer" subject in nineteenth-century fiction. First of all, he benefited from an implied relation between his Indian feature and the *idea* of the noble savage. It is true, of course, that there were countercurrents. The most evident of these was a frontier sentiment equating the red and black races, typified by the expression "red niggers" in Bird's *Nick of the Woods* (1837), but also seen in Aiken's *The Indian Mazeppa* (1878) and *Talbot in Apache Land* (1892). Occasionally the Indian was even ranked below the Negro, exemplified by a remark in Caroline Kirkland's *Western Clearings* (1846): "Some people pretend to think niggers haven't got souls, . . . they have; as for Indians, it's all nonsense!"[3] But these views were balanced by the prevalent noble savage pattern in nineteenth-century fiction. This legendary nobility informed, among others, Rowson's, Stephens's, Neal's, Snelling's, Arrington's, Jackson's, and Ingraham's management of their half-blood characters. They were relatively comfortable with their racial hybrids because of the convention of the noble savage, whereas the mulatto shared in the ignobility attributed to the black slave by the contemporary *idea* of the Negro, an ignobility even the abolitionist movement found difficult to deny.

A second factor accounting for the half-blood's literary viability was the impression among white settlers and readers that the Indian was moving toward extinction, a belief explicitly expressed in such works as Cooper's *The Last of the Mohicans*, Whitman's "The Half-Breed," and Jackson's *Ramona*. In the popular imagination, as Pearce has shown, the Indian was safely entombed in history or in prehistory. The mixed-blood Indian, of course, was immediately present, menacingly so to many white settlers early in the century; but at some unconscious level of white perception, an analogy was drawn between incipient Indian extinction and intrinsic half-blood genetic deficiency. In spite of deep-seated fears to the contrary, white authors gave the impression that just as the red race was irreversibly declining before the advance of civilization, so too would the Indian side of the half-blood become increasingly recessive, diluted through the generations until its latent (symbolic) capacity to erupt in the midst of civilization dwindled away.

Thus, ambivalently, Snelling refined his half-breed protagonist, Child removed the Indian father and the name of her fictional mixed-blood, and Rowson made her quarter-blood renounce his Indian heritage. Frequently in nineteenth-century American fiction the half-blood dies, either actually or symbolically. Symbolic deaths include such literary strategies as the removal of the half-blood from America (he or she usually goes to Mexico, as evidenced in Ingraham's *The Phantom Mazeppa* and Jackson's *Ramona*) or the bifurcation of the mixed-blood in a manner suggesting the demise of his Indian heritage (e.g., Child's *Hobomok*, Snelling's "The Bois Brulé," Jones's *Bloody Brook*, and Aiken's *The Indian Mazeppa*).

While the Indian was declining, however, in the white American imagination and in fact the Negro was emerging. In contrast to the red race, the black race was thought to be proliferating, its ever-increasing number a possible and likely threat not only to the present but especially to the future of (white) civilization in America. Unlike the declining red side of the half-blood, the black component of the mulatto reminded whites of what they regarded as the menace of black dominance, of the peril of an increasingly subversive and ignoble presence within society and possibly within future white progeny.

This fear of black proliferation relates to a third reason why American authors exercised greater artistic freedom in treating half-blood than mulatto characters. In the nineteenth century and earlier, Indians are described as affectively cold, as barely capable of reproducing themselves. Blacks, on the other hand, are portrayed as carnally promiscuous, as frightfully fecund. The literature of the period is replete with observations in support of this generalization, but William Gilmore Simms's "Caloya," a story printed in *The Wigwam and the Cabin* (1845), provides a telling example. The story concerns Mingo, a black driver who is "a ladies' man" and who is said to have many wives on various plantations. He is attracted to Caloya, an Indian maiden "whom he thought destined to provoke his jaded tastes anew, and restore his passions to their primitive ascendancy."[4] He tries to purchase her from Richard Knuckles, her husband, then tries to seduce her, even tries to rape her when all else fails. Simms leaves no doubt about Mingo's sexual prowess, which is contrasted with that of the Indian, who loves but cannot love "with the ardour of the white": "Civilization is prolific, barbarism sterile. The dweller in the city has more various appetites and more active passions than the dweller in the camp, and the habits of the hunter, lead, above all things, to an intense gathering up of all things in self; a practice which tends, necessarily, to that sort of independence which is, perhaps, neither more nor less than one aspect of barrenness" (p. 378).

As we have seen in *The Partisan* and *Mellichampe*, Simms depicts the red and black races as equally beneath the white race, and "Caloya" emphasizes "the inferior moral sense and sensibility of both Indian and negro" (p. 410). Because whites are not involved in the central action of the story, Simms can treat the southern fear of miscegenation directly, in obvious contrast to his oblique management of Mother Blonay's curse in *The Partisan*. There is safety, for Simms, in presenting the theme in terms of red and black protagonists,[5] Simms's horror all too evident in the interaction between sensual Mingo and phlegmatic Knuckles. The anti-miscegenation theme of the story draws energy from Simms's perception of the incongruity of Mingo's attachment to Caloya: "His race is more prolific, and, by increasing rather than diminishing, multiply necessarily, and unhappily, the great sinfulness of mankind" (p. 411). Simms puts his finger, as it were, on the pulse of the greater freedom, however ambivalent and restricted, authors experienced in writing of the half-blood; unlike the black side of the mulatto, the red feature of the half-blood was waning.

This unconscious analogy between the decline of the red race and the implied recessive nature of the half-blood's Indian blood becomes apparent as well in observations during the century about Tituba, the Carib Indian who was the first to confess in the Salem witchcraft trials. In Henry Wadsworth Longfellow's play *Giles Corey of the Salem Farms* (1868), in George Bancroft's *History of the United States* (revised edition, 1876), and in John Gorham Palfrey's *History of New England* (1877), Tituba is said to have been half-Indian and half-Negro.[6] The equation of the red and black races in this development is interesting, but the significant feature lies in the apparent need in the second half of the century to revitalize Tituba's threatening image by amalgamating her Indian heritage with the black race. In the 1860s and 1870s the Indian was indeed on the decline—by 1845 eastern Indians had been reduced or removed to reservations west of the Mississippi River—whereas after the Civil War the black was emergent; and Tituba's hold on the American imagination as an evil force was maintained in the second half of the nineteenth century by white society's tendency to identify her less with the Indian and more with the Negro.

The threat of black potency, either in sexual reproduction or in its surrogate, witchcraft, included the race's increasing spatial presence. In the South the black was prominent on the plantation and even in the master's home, as servant and parent figure. In the North he was (theoretically at least) a free citizen, mingling at will among whites. The Indians, in contrast, were not only declining in numbers but, steadily during the century, confined to reservations in the West. The decline of the Indian in number and in physical presence, as opposed to the increasing visibility of the Negro in white society, permitted authors to feel greater comfort with half-blood than with mulatto characters.

An important fifth factor should not be overlooked. The "Indian problem" never divided America into factions equivalent in force and effect to the "black problem." America's difficulties with the red race never amounted to anything like the Civil War. The facts that the Indian was vanishing, that he was safely confined to reservations, that he represented an ailing minority lent hope, at some level of the white American mind, to the impression that the prevalence of half-bloods on the frontier would also pass away, that with the increasing scarcity of pure Indian blood the red taint of the half-blood would eventually become diluted over the generations until its presence would be insignificant. Of course, as we have seen in Melville's *The Confidence-Man* and elsewhere, white Americans of the century feared the implications of this savage taint, which might uncontrollably erupt and fracture social order; but the fear lessened as the century lengthened, and in fact late nineteenth-century fiction generally portrays quarter-bloods benignly and romantically. In contrast, the fear of the taint of black blood intensified as, during the century, blacks seemed to reproduce abundantly, became increasingly spatially apparent, and attained the freedom to mingle as equals with whites. Future generations would not necessarily reduce the primitive black side of the mulatto, for the pure black was all too prominent and would be even more so in the future. As the nightmare of Poe's *The Narrative of Arthur Gordon Pym* intimates, there was thought to be the distinct possibility that in time primitive black blood would infiltrate the white race to the extent that the civilized pure-blood white might become a receding minority.

The half-blood may have been a "safer" fictional protagonist than the mulatto, but, as the writers of the century indicate, he always remained an enigma: "half Indian, half white man, and half devil." He was more than the sum of his parts, an impression underlying the pervasive ambivalence with which he was portrayed in the fiction of the period. Yet this very ambiguity made him a viable literary subject, even in southern writings in which he was often most stereotypically presented.

Nineteenth-century American writers participated in a universal cultural experience, one in which a group of people was marginalized even while it served—perhaps so that it *could* serve—as a creative resource for the dominant group. Such "betwixt-and-between" marginal experiences, to apply Victor Turner's concept, at once disconcertingly revealed the concealed premises of the established white culture and paradoxically revitalized that culture's sense of communal structure.[7] Literally, as we have seen, half-bloods were held in suspicion and opprobrium by the very same white settlers who depended upon them in essential life-supportive ways; in fiction, half-bloods similarly served as mediators between man (the half-blood's white heritage) and nature (his red heritage). Like stigma-typed groups in general,[8] half-bloods existed, in the writer's imagination, somewhere between civilized white and primitive red culture; or, if we speak anthropologically, the half-blood represented a form of pollution or disorder which included a danger to existing social patterns as well as a potential power to transform and energize those patterns.[9] As Parkman's anecdotal remark implies when it alludes to the image of the fallen angel, the half-blood's enigmatic mediatory place as a new species between primitivism and civilization manifests at once his capacity for subhuman depravity and superhuman potentiality. Fictional portraits of the half-blood oscillated between these extremes, with southern accounts tending more toward the subhuman sphere and with northern accounts tending more toward superhuman promise. He indeed became, as Irving referred to him, a frontier Robin Hood, paradoxically an outlaw (his subhuman side) benefiting (his superhuman side) a society otherwise helpless.

Whether sub- or superhuman, the half-blood linked civilization and nature in a vital way, made the primal energies of nature available to civilization and kept white society alive both physically on the frontier and spiritually or vicariously in fiction. By simultaneously embodying the antithesis and the epitome of human possibility, he reinvigorated American society's sense of itself, particularly of its relation to the idea of America's promise established during the seventeenth and eighteenth centuries. We see this in Neal's *Rachel Dyer*, for example, but also in such disparate works as Rowson's *Reuben and Rachel* and Simms's *The Partisan*. This reinvigoration is illustrated *par excellence* in the half-blood in spirit, the pure-blood white character who, in every respect save genetic, functioned creatively between civilization (white) and nature (red) as if he or she were an actual half-blood. This revitalization of white social identity emanated from writers' exploration of the dialectic features of the half-blood in fact and of his surrogate, the half-blood in spirit. In the American phenomenon of this hybrid species, as opposed to the mulatto, authors could dramatize with relative comfort the dynamics of the human self, with its tension between rationality and savagery, as well as of society, with its tension between order and chaos—most especially of society in nineteenth-century America, an unsettled land uniting a civilized East and a primitive West. Through him, rather than through the mulatto, writers felt free to experiment with the artistic management of themes and symbols related to the dynamics of the self, of society, and of America.

For a variety of reasons, some cultural and some authorial, fictional treatments of the half-blood are on the whole artistic failures. Yet, as myopic and incapacitated as many of these accounts appear, their authors did see something artistically fascinating in the mixed-blood; and what they saw in the half-blood and how they expressed it resulted in the creation of an instructive cultural symbol in nineteenth-century American fiction.

Notes ❧

PREFACE

1. James Axtell, "The Ethnohistory of Early America: A Review Essay," *William and Mary Quarterly* 35 (1978): 140–41.

2. The idea of the "noble savage," the view of the Indian as living in harmony with nature's laws through reason and instinct in an idealized primitivism, is a complex concept which underwent degrees of change. For a review of the notion, see Robert F. Berkhofer, Jr., *The White Man's Indian: Images of the American Indian from Columbus to the Present* (New York, 1978).

CHAPTER ONE

1. Edwin Fussell, *Frontier: American Literature and the American West* (Princeton, 1965), pp. 6, 15.

2. Roy Harvey Pearce, *The Savages of America: A Study of the Indian and the Idea of Civilization* (Baltimore, 1965), p. 194.

3. See, among others, Henry Nash Smith, *Virgin Land: The American West as Symbol and Myth* (Cambridge, Mass., 1950).

4. Albert Keiser, *The Indian in American Literature* (New York, 1933), p. 296.

5. Alexander Ross, *The Fur Hunters of the Far West*, ed. Kenneth A. Spaulding (Norman, Okla., 1956), pp. 196–98.

6. Alexander Ross, *The Red River Settlement* (London, 1856), pp. 193, 23, 242.

7. A. Irving Hallowell, "American Indians, White and Black: The Phenomenon of Transculturation," *Contributions to Anthropology* (Chicago, 1976), pp. 498–529.

8. W. H. Emory, *Report on the United States and Mexican Boundary Survey, Made under the Direction of the Secretary of the Interior* (Washington, D.C., 1857), 1:69.

9. A recent study contends that after 1850, pity and contempt for squaw men gave way to envy and hostility because these individuals were flourishing on the closed reservation; see William T. Hagan, "Squaw Men

on the Kiowa, Comanche, and Apache Reservation: Advance Agents of Civilization or Disturbers of the Peace?" in *The Frontier Challenge: Responses to the Trans-Mississippi West*, ed. John G. Clark (Lawrence, Kan., 1971), p. 197.

10. See, for instance, James E. Seaver, *A Narrative of the Life of Mary Jemison* [1824] (New York, 1910), p. 67; and Lewis O. Saum, *The Fur Trader and the Indian* (Seattle, 1965), p. 85. Apparently some Indian women saw marriage to whites as a form of social improvement: see Bernard De Voto, *Across the Wide Missouri* (Boston, 1947), pp. 99–101.

11. Timothy Flint, *Recollections of the Last Ten Years in the Valley of the Mississippi*, ed. George R. Brooks (Carbondale and Edwardsville, Ill., 1968), pp. 97, 119.

12. See, for instance, Francis Parkman, *The Oregon Trail*, ed. E. N. Feltskog (Madison, 1969), p. 76; and James Hall, *Sketches of History, Life, and Manners in the West* (Philadelphia, 1835), 1:76. Other pertinent passages will become apparent in the course of this study.

13. Clark Wissler, *Indian Cavalcade* (New York, 1938), p. 236. Identity problems, aggravated by the hatred of his white stepfather, plagued the half-blood child of the Smith family of Mill Creek in western Virginia, and when he became old enough he ran away to join the Indians (Willis De Hass, *History of the Early Settlement and Indian Wars of Western Virginia* [Wheeling, W. Va., 1851], pp. 205–06).

14. Chandler Gilman, *Life on the Lakes: Being Tales and Sketches Collected During a Trip to the Pictured Rocks of Lake Superior* (New York, 1836), 2:100, 98–99.

15. Bernard Sheehan, *Seeds of Extinction: Jeffersonian Philanthropy and the American Indian* (Chapel Hill, N.C., 1975), p. 162.

16. See D. T. Campbell, "Stereotypes and the Perception of Group Differences," *American Psychologist* 22 (1967): 817–29.

17. Hallowell, "American Indians," pp. 498–529.

18. Seaver, *Life of Mary Jemison*, p. 131. See also James Axtell, "The White Indian of Colonial America," *William and Mary Quarterly* 32 (1975): 62–63. To Francis Parkman, half-bloods "seemed to aim at assimilating themselves to their red associates" (*Oregon Trail*, p. 176). An unusual instance of Indian hostility toward the mixed-blood is reported by Maximilian, Prince of Weed, in *Travels in the Interior of North America, 1832–1834*, vol. 23 of *Early Western Travels, 1748–1846*, ed. Reuben Gold Thwaites (Cleveland, 1906), p. 383.

19. Apparently Pitchlynn was actually a quarter blood; see W. David Baird, *Peter Pitchlynn: Chief of the Choctaws* (Norman, Okla., 1972), p. 19. According to legend, but apparently not in fact, Osceola of the Seminoles

was a mixed-blood Indian. It is interesting to note that between 1870 and 1900 a large proportion of Negro political leaders were mulattoes, quadroons, or octoroons; see Clement Eaton, *The Mind of the Old South* (Baton Rouge, La., 1967), p. 192.

20. *Indian Treaties: 1778–1883*, ed. Charles J. Kappler (New York, 1972), passim.

21. See Robert F. Berkhofer, Jr., *Salvation and the Savage: An Analysis of Protestant Missions and American Indian Response, 1787–1862* (Lexington, Ky., 1965), pp. 112–13.

22. See Ronald N. Satz, *American Indian Policy in the Jacksonian Era* (Lincoln, Nebr., 1975), pp. 67–71. See also Edmund Jefferson Danziger, Jr., *Indians and Bureaucrats: Administering the Reservation Policy during the Civil War* (Urbana, Ill., 1974), p. 169; George E. Hyde, *Spotted Tail's Folk: A History of the Brulé Sioux* (Norman, Okla., 1961), pp. 288, 290–91. A half-blood is the spokesman for a tribal remnant in Thomas Nuttall's *A Journal of Travels into the Arkansa Territory During the Year 1819*, vol. 13 of *Early Western Travels* (Cleveland, 1905), p. 182. And in *The Memoirs of Chief Red Fox* (New York, 1971), a half-blood named Charlie Reynolds is said to have betrayed to the whites the full-blooded Indian who had avenged the death of Eagle Shield, which led to Rain-in-the-Face's arrest and cruel treatment by General George Armstrong Custer (p. 38).

23. Flint, *Recollections*, p. 108.

24. M. B. Brewer, "Determinants of Social Distance among East African Tribal Units," *Journal of Personality and Social Psychology* 15 (1970): 179–89.

25. The tendency is evident in numerous accounts and is exemplified, for instance, in Charles McKnight's *Our Western Border* [1875] (Philadelphia, 1879), pp. 554–61.

26. Ross, *Red River Settlement*, pp. 362–86.

27. Ibid., pp. 239, 190, 191–92.

28. Wissler, *Indian Cavalcade*, p. 232; Saum, *Fur Trader*, p. 209.

29. John K. Townsend, *Narrative of a Journey across the Rocky Mountains, to the Columbia River* [1839], vol. 21 of *Early Western Travels* (Cleveland, 1905), p. 213.

30. Elizabeth Fries Ellet, *Summer Rambles in the West* (New York, 1853), p. 50.

31. Ross, *Red River Settlement*, p. 232.

32. Emory, *Report*, 1:69.

33. See Julian Huxley, *Eugenics and Society* (London, 1936), p. 167; Ruth Benedict, *Race: Science and Politics* (New York, 1943), p. 78; and Wissler, *Indian Cavalcade*, p. 236. One recent physical anthropologist,

however, argues that great diversity of ancestry results in lower fertility: J. B. Bresler, "The Relationship between the Fertility Pattern of the F_1 Generation and the Number of Countries of Birth Represented in the F_1 Generation," *American Journal of Physical Anthropology* 20 (1962): 509–13.

34. My observations on this work originally appeared in greater detail in "Frontier Robin Hood: Wilderness, Civilization and the Half-Breed in Irving's *A Tour on the Prairies*," *Southwestern American Literature* 4 (1974): 14–21.

35. Washington Irving, *A Tour on the Prairies* (New York, 1967), p. 3. Text references are to this edition. For a survey of the response to this work by Irving's contemporaries, see Martha Dula, "Audience Response to *A Tour on the Prairies* in 1835," *Western American Literature* 8 (1973): 67–74.

36. Washington Irving, *The Sketch Book*, (New York, 1869), p. 18.

37. Washington Irving, *Astoria* (New York, 1868), p. 19. In *Astoria* Irving likewise frequently compares the frontier to "the wastes of the ocean or the deserts of Arabia" (p. 217).

38. Irving, *Sketch Book*, pp. 14, 15.

39. Irving, *Astoria*, p. 217.

40. Ibid., p. 16.

41. Irving, *Astoria*, p. 119; *The Adventures of Captain Bonneville, U.S.A. in the Rocky Mountains and the Far West* (New York, 1869), p. 85.

42. C. Merton Babcock suggests that, at least in Chapter Twenty of *A Tour*, Irving refers to horses allegorically (*The American Frontier: A Social and Literary Record* [New York, 1965], p. 169). See also William Bedford Clark, "How the West Won: Irving's Comic Inversion of the Westering Myth in *A Tour on the Prairies*," *American Literature* 50 (1978): 347.

43. *The Western Journals of Washington Irving*, ed. John Francis McDermott (Norman, Okla., 1944).

44. Wayne Kime, "The Completeness of Washington Irving's *A Tour on the Prairies*," *Western American Literature* 8 (1973): 55–65.

45. On Irving's tendency to romanticize in *A Tour*, see Edgeley W. Todd, "Washington Irving Discovers the Frontier," *Western Humanities Review* 11 (1957): 29–39; and Robert Edson Lee, *From West to East: Studies in the Literature of the American West* (Urbana, Ill., 1966), pp. 68–69. Thomas J. Lyon has observed that Irving's description of the effect of the frontier on people is more successful than his depiction of the land: "Washington Irving's Wilderness," *Western American Literature* 1 (1966): 168–74. Sir Walter Scott's use of the Robin Hood motif as exemplary of the popular romantic naturalization or taming of the outlaw, and the

motif's influence on Cooper are discussed by Leslie A. Fielder, *Love and Death in the American Novel* (Cleveland, 1962), pp. 154–71.

46. Irving, *Astoria*, pp. 141, 217. Pierre Dorion, the half-blood interpreter in this narrative, does not serve as a nexus for the forces of civilization and the wilderness, as Beatte did in *A Tour*.

47. Irving, *Bonneville*, p. 422.

48. Herman Melville, *The Confidence-Man* (New York, 1857), p. 231. In Chapter Twelve, the man with the weed is said to have a half-blood daughter, but we are told nothing about her. In Chapter Seventeen, we encounter another lonely man with his apparent daughter, who is walking in moccasins and is "evidently of alien maternity, perhaps Creole, or even Comanche" (p. 130).

49. This inherent antagonism between the self and society relates to the theme, in *The Confidence-Man*, of love and hate as antagonistic yet inherent components in Christianity, and to the ironic portrait in the novel of the best haters as the best Christians; on this theme see Hershel Parker, "The Metaphysics of Indian-Hating," *Nineteenth-Century Fiction* 18 (1963): 165–73. In a review of *The California and Oregon Trail* Melville denounced Francis Parkman's Indian racism: "We are all of us—Anglo-Saxons, Dyaks, and Indians—sprung from one head, and made in one image. . . . And wherever we recognize the image of God, let us reverence it, though it hung from the gallows" (*The Literary World* 4 [31 March 1849]:291).

50. Flint, *Recollections*, p. 120.

51. Alexis de Tocqueville, *Democracy in America*, ed. J. P. Mayer (Garden City, N.Y., 1969), pp. 329, 356. A brief, favorable English observation about an encounter with a half-blood appears in a letter published in the *Christian Observer* (London) and later reprinted as an appendix to Adam Hodgson's *Remarks During a Journey Through North America* (New York, 1823), pp. 278–80. Foreign novelists, as we shall see—such writers as the Englishman Mayne Reid and the Frenchman Oliver Gloux—treated the half-blood more positively than did their American contemporaries.

52. Parkman, *Oregon Trail*, p. 315.

CHAPTER TWO

1. James McKenzie, "The King's Posts and Journal of a Canoe Jaunt through the King's Domains, 1808," in L. R. Masson, *Les Bourgeois de la Compagnie du Nord-Ouest* (New York, 1960), 2:421.

2. John Ross Browne, "A Dangerous Journey," *Crusoe's Island: A Ramble in the Footsteps of Alexander Selkirk* (New York, 1864), p. 238. Text references are to this edition.

3. *Selected Writings of Edgar Allan Poe*, ed. Edward H. Davidson (Boston, 1956), pp. 280, 287, 295. A good discussion of Dirk Peters appears in Joseph J. Moldenhauer's "Imagination and Perversity in *The Narrative of Arthur Gordon Pym*," *Texas Studies in Literature and Language* 13 (1971): 267–80.

4. This interpretation is most recently reiterated in *Race and the American Romantics*, ed. Vincent Freimarck and Bernard Rosenthal (New York, 1971), pp. 2–3.

5. Mary Howard, *The Black Gauntlet: A Tale of Plantation Life in South Carolina* (Philadelphia, 1860), pp. vii, 86. Text references are to this edition.

6. James W. Steele, *The Sons of the Border: Sketches of the Life and People of the Far Frontier* (Topeka, Kans., 1872), p. 51. Text references are to this edition. As for the frequency of racial interbreeding in this region, Josiah Gregg remarked in 1844 that "the present race of New Mexicans has . . . become an amalgam, averaging about equal parts of the European and aboriginal blood" (*Commerce of the Prairies* [Indianapolis, 1970], p. 71).

7. No half-breeds appear in *Old Hicks, the Guide; or, Adventures in the Comanche Country in Search of a Gold Mine* (New York, 1848). In the particular episode to which I refer a brother recognizes his sister by means of a crucifix which had been their mother's.

8. *Mark Twain's Works* (New York, 1923), 1:267, 100. "Huck Finn and Tom Sawyer among the Indians" (ca. 1884) suggests Clemens's hostile attitude toward Indians in general; see *Mark Twain's Hannibal, Huck & Tom*, ed. Walter Blair (Berkeley, Cal., 1969), pp. 81–140.

9. *Mark Twain's Works*, 1:236. Most recently, Tom H. Towers has intelligently discussed Injun Joe's function in the novel: "'I Never Thought We Might Want to Come Back': Strategies of Transcendence in *Tom Sawyer*," *Modern Fiction Studies* 21 (1975–1976), 509–20. Arthur G. Pettit mentions, very briefly, that Injun Joe's threat against the Widow Douglas represents the racial violence Clemens sees beneath the pastoral camouflage of St. Petersburg (*Mark Twain and the South* [Lexington, Ky., 1974], pp. 59–60). On one occasion Clemens jokingly refers to himself as "only an ignorant half-breed" ("The Old Pah-Utah," *Mark Twain of the Enterprise: Newspaper Articles and Other Documents, 1862–1864*, ed. Henry Nash Smith [Berkeley, Cal., 1952], p. 99).

10. George Catlin, *Catlin's Notes of Eight Years' Travel and Residence in Europe* (London, 1848), p. 153.

11. James Burchett Ransom, *Osceola; or, Fact and Fiction* (New York, 1838), p. 15. Text references are to this edition.

12. Alfred W. Arrington, *The Rangers and Regulators of the Tanaha: or, Life among the Lawless. A Tale of the Republic of Texas* (New York, 1856), pp. 44; repeated on p. 88. The novel was published under the pseudonym Charles Summerfield. Text references are to this edition.

13. Joseph Crosswell, *A New World Planted; or, The Adventures of the Forefathers of New-England; Who Landed in Plymouth, December 22, 1620* (Boston, 1802), p. 20. As an aside, Pocahontas's son, Thomas Rolfe, returned to Virginia in the 1630s and contributed to the virtual annihilation of his mother's people.

14. Prentiss Ingraham, *The Phantom Mazeppa; or, The Hyena of the Chaparrals: A Romance of Love and Adventure on the Nebraska Plains* (New York, 1882), p. 3. Text references are to this edition. See also Ingraham's *Buffalo Bill's Trackers; or, A Man of His Word* (New York, 1908).

15. In contrast to its ennoblement of Ingraham's Sancho, the presence of Aztec blood accounts for the murderous behavior of the heroine of *For the Soul of Rafael* (1906) by turn-of-the-century author Marah Ellis Ryan.

16. See Frederick Merk, *Manifest Destiny and Mission in American History* (New York, 1963).

17. *The Complete Works of Kate Chopin*, ed. Per Seyersted (Baton Rouge, La., 1969), 1:212. Text references are to this edition.

18. See Per Seyersted, *Kate Chopin: A Critical Biography* (Baton Rouge, La., 1969), pp. 93–98.

19. As suggested in J. V. Ridgely's *William Gilmore Simms* (New York, 1962), p. 66.

20. William Gilmore Simms, *The Partisan: A Romance of the Revolution* (New York, 1859), p. 96. Text references are to this edition. My discussion will focus on Goggle's role in this romance rather than in its sequel because the symbolic dimension of Goggle is carefully established there by Simms.

21. An interpretation suggested in passing by Simone Vauthier, "Of Time and the South: The Fiction of William Gilmore Simms," *Southern Literary Journal* 5 (1972): 17.

22. Roy Harvey Pearce discusses Simms's identification of Indians and Negroes (*The Savages of America: The Study of the Indian and the Idea of Civilization* [Baltimore, 1965], pp. 216–20). Of tangential interest is Elmo Howell's "William Gilmore Simms and the American Indian," *South Carolina Review* 5 (1974): 57–64.

23. Transposition of motif, so as to convey symbolic meaning by association, is one neglected feature of the art Simms practiced. For a discussion of how Simms relates swamp imagery to the colonials and hurricane

imagery to the British invaders, see L. Moffitt Cecil's "Functional Imagery in Simms's *The Partisan*," in *Studies in Medieval, Renaissance, American Literature* (Fort Worth, Tex., 1971), pp. 155–64.

24. On Simms's landscape imagery, see Annette Kolodny, "The Unchanging Landscape: The Pastoral Impulse in Simms's Revolutionary War Romances," *Southern Literary Journal* 5 (1972):46–67.

25. The quotations in this paragraph are from *The Wigwam and the Cabin* (New York, 1856), pp. 46, 47.

26. *The Yemassee: A Romance of Carolina* (New York, 1853), p. 325.

27. *Partisan*, p. x.

CHAPTER THREE

1. Alexander Ross, *The Fur Hunters of the Far West*, ed. Kenneth A. Spaulding (Norman, Okla., 1956), p. 196.

2. Robert Montgomery Bird, *A Belated Revenge: From the Papers of Ipsico Poe*, in *Lippincott's Magazine* 44 (1889):604–05.

3. Ibid., pp. 621, 657, 658. Curtis Dahl mentions in passing, probably too certainly, that Craven is a half-blood (*Robert Montgomery Bird* [New York, 1963], p. 103). In "Awossagame, or the Seal of the Evil One," an unpublished story preserved in manuscript in the University of Pennsylvania Library, Bird presents a young woman who seems to be "a half-breed savage," "mongrel scum of Indian and French blood" (pp. 15, 27). To the relief of everyone concerned (especially Elliot Sherwyn, who would marry her were she not partially savage), she is in fact Elizabeth Gilbert, Judge Gilbert's daughter who had disappeared seventeen years ago when she was six months of age.

4. The theme of innocence in Bird's *Nick of the Woods*, a novel written in the same year, is discussed in R. W. B. Lewis, *The American Adam: Innocence, Tragedy, and Tradition in the Nineteenth Century* (Chicago, 1955), pp. 105–09.

5. For a controversial study of this recurrent theme in American literature (though *A Belated Revenge* is not discussed) see Richard Slotkin, *Regeneration through Violence: The Mythology of the American Frontier, 1600–1860* (Middletown, Conn., 1973).

6. Dahl, *Robert Montgomery Bird*, pp. 59, 109.

7. The story was first published in *The Aristidean* 1 (1845): 36–64. An earlier version of my remarks on this story appeared in "Whitman's Grotesque Half-Breed," *Walt Whitman Review* 23 (1977): 133–36.

8. See Thomas Ollive Mabbott, ed., *The Half-Breed and Other Stories by Walt Whitman* (New York, 1927), p. 13; Joseph Jay Ruben, *The Historic Whitman* (University Park, Pa., 1973), pp. 120–21; and Floyd Stovall, *The Foreground of "Leaves of Grass"* (Charlottesville, Va., 1974), pp. 38–

41. Autobiographical elements in the story are mentioned by Mabbott, p. 13; Katherine Molinoff, *Monographs on Unpublished Whitman Material* (New York, 1941), no. 2, pp. 3–4; and Florence Bernstein Friedman, *Walt Whitman Looks at the Schools* (New York, 1950), p. 35.

9. In the Brooklyn *Daily Eagle*, 1–6, 8, 9 June 1846.

10. Whitman's racial views remain unclear; in spite of Leadie M. Clark's carefully documented *Walt Whitman's Concept of the American Common Man* (New York, 1955), some critics still participate in an unfocused dialogue on the subject. Compare Freimarck and Rosenthal's recent *Race and the American Romantics* (New York, 1971), p. 36, with Jerome M. Loving's *Civil War Letters of George Washington Whitman* (Durham, N.C., 1975), p. 5. "The Half-Breed" will not settle the controversy, but it does provide a glint of insight into Whitman's early racial views.

11. Clark, *Walt Whitman's Concept*, p. 56.

12. *Walt Whitman: The Early Poems and the Fiction*, ed. Thomas L. Brasher (New York, 1963), p. 287. Text references are to this edition.

13. In "Prohibition of Colored Persons," Brooklyn *Daily Times*, 6 May 1858; see Freimarck and Rosenthal, *Race and the American Romantics*, pp. 46–47. See also Clark, *Whitman's Concept*, p. 51; and Whitman's "Black and White Slaves," New York *Aurora*, 2 April 1842, reprinted in *Unpublished Poetry and Prose of Walt Whitman*, ed. Emory Holloway (New York, 1921), 2:183.

14. The portrait of Boddo and his malicious deeds call for his death at the end of the story; but the story's concern with capital punishment prevented Whitman from performing "poetic justice." To remain consistent with his view of capital punishment, he permits the half-blood to escape to a life of misery.

15. Apparently Whitman's first likely opportunity to encounter half-bloods, at least in their natural habitat, was during his trip to New Orleans in February 1848.

16. At the end of the second chapter of his *Walt Whitman's Champion: William Douglas O'Connor* (College Station, Tex., 1977).

17. Stovall remarks on Whitman's knowledge of Simms's writings (*Foreground*, p. 122).

18. *Silver-spur; or, the Mountain Heroine. A Tale of the Arapaho Country* (New York, 1870), p. 97.

19. Oliver Gloux, *The White Scalper: A Story of the Texan War* (New York, 1881), p. 21. The novel was published under the pseudonym Gustave Aimard.

20. Henry R. Sienkiewicz, *Western Septet: Seven Stories of the American West*, trans. Marion Moore Coleman (Cheshire, Conn., 1973), p. 89.

21. *The Writings of Thomas Jefferson*, ed. Albert Ellery Bergh (Wash-

ington, D.C., 1907), 16:452. Cf. a letter written 6 December 1813 (11: 353–54). A century earlier, another southerner, William Byrd, argued that if whites could "stomach" marrying Indians, desirable pragmatic results would emerge. Through intermarriage with whites, the Indians' dark complexion and paganism would be supplanted, as well as their friendship and their land secured by the white race (*Histories of the Dividing Line Between Virginia and North Carolina*, ed. William K. Boyd [New York, 1967], pp. 3–4). Apparently this southern minority sentiment, evident in Virginians Byrd and Jefferson, originates from John Rolfe's marriage to Pocahontas in the seventeenth-century, a marriage which was justified by practical reasons of the sort suggested by Byrd and which was soon transformed from a dubious undertaking to benign legend.

22. For the story of Eunice Williams, see J. Norman Heard, *White into Red: A Study of the Assimilation of White Persons Captured by Indians* (Metuchen, N.J., 1973), pp. 19–21.

23. Lydia Maria Child, *Hobomok* (Boston, 1824), p. 46. Text references are to this edition. Information about many of the female authors I mention can be found in Nina Baym's *Woman's Fiction: A Guide to Novels by and about Women in America, 1820–1870* (Ithaca, N.Y., 1978).

24. It is common in the fiction of this period that when a white person, usually a male, marries a member of the red race, the latter is abandoned at the end for another Caucasian individual, who most frequently has been previously thought to be dead. See, for instance, George F. Ruxton's novel, *Life in the Far West* (New York, 1849).

25. Lydia Maria Child, *Letters from New-York* (New York, 1843), p. 250; idem, *Fact and Fiction: A Collection of Stories* (New York, 1846), pp. 61–76.

26. James Kirke Paulding, *Koningsmarke, the Long Finne: A Story of the New World* (London, 1839), p. 74.

27. Susanna Hoswell Rowson, *Reuben and Rachel* (Boston, 1798), pp. 168, 169. Text references are to this edition. In *The Vision of Columbus: A Poem in Nine Books* (Hartford, Conn., 1787) Joel Barlow suggests that in time American Indians will lighten and the white settlers will darken (p. 53), but the implied miscegenation with its symbolic mixed-blood overtones remains vague in the poem.

28. Helen Hunt Jackson, *Ramona: A Story* (New York, 1912), pp. 35, 147, 155. Text references are to this edition.

29. See Franklin Walker's discussion of the flaws in the novel in *A Literary History of Southern California* (Berkeley, Cal., 1950), pp. 123–32.

30. Mayne Reid, *The Wild Huntress* (New York, 1882), p. 4. Similar favorable treatment is given to Pawnee Bill, a quarter-blood, in John W.

Osburn's *The Brand-Burners of Cimarron; or, Detective Goldspur's Pard* (New York, 1897).

31. Mayne Reid, *The White Squaw* (New York, 1883), p. 6. Text references are to this edition. In collaboration with Frederick Whittaker, Reid also presents a positive portrait of a minor half-blood character in *The Wild-Horse Hunters* (New York, 1877).

32. John G. Neihardt, *Indian Tales and Others* (New York, 1926), pp. 118, 123. Text references are to this edition. An unnamed half-blood woman, whose only virtues apparently are her beauty and her virginity, destroys the friendship of Will Carpenter and Mike Fink (and inadvertently of Mike Fink and Frank Talbeau) in Neihardt's hundred-page poem, *The Song of Three Friends* (New York, 1919). Another midwesterner, Thomas Chalmers Harbaugh, briefly presents a good-hearted half-blood named Monte but, typically, has him quickly murdered in *Navajo Nick, the Boy Gold Hunter; or the Three Pards of the Basaltic Buttes. A Tale of Arizona* (Cleveland, 1886), pp. 47–48. And Samuel S. Hall, an easterner who spent some time and acquired a reputation in Texas, ambivalently presents Francisco Flores, a swarthy half-blood who is "villainous in appearance" but who volunteers information about a desperado's plot for reasons not entirely clear but presumably in part for an anticipated reward: *Little Lone Star; or, the Belle of the Cibolo* (New York, 1886), p. 6. See also Hall's *Chiota, the Creek; or the Three Thunderbolts* (New York, 1884).

33. Edward S. Ellis, *The Hunted Hunter; or, the Strange Horseman of the Prairie. A Romance of the South-west Border* (New York, 1880), pp. 2, 16; and (under the pseudonym Latham C. Carleton) *Scar-Cheek, the Wild Half-Breed; or, Chase after the Savages of the Frontier* (Cleveland, 1909), pp. 34–35. Text references to *The Half-Blood; or, the Panther of the Plains* (New York, 1882) appear parenthetically in the text.

34. William Manning, *Texas Chick, the Southwest Detective; or, Tiger-Lily, the Vulture Queen* (New York, 1884), p. 6. Text references are to this edition (published under the pseudonym Mark Wilton).

35. Edward L. Wheeler, *Bob Woolf, the Border Ruffian; or, the Girl Dead-Shot* (New York, 1899), p. 1. Wheeler probably died in 1885, but his name continued to appear on new novels long after this date.

36. Idem, *Sierra Sam, the Detective: A Tale of Fairy Flats* (New York, 1900), pp. 2–3. Albert W. Aiken's *The Fresh on the Rio Grande* (New York, 1887) and *Lone Hand, the Shadow* (New York, 1889) present typical Jewish characters.

37. Edward L. Wheeler, *Nobby Nick of Nevada; or, the Scamp of the Sierras* (New York, 1899), p. 21.

38. Two noteworthy exceptions are Roy Harvey Pearce, who devotes

a few pages to the work in *The Savages of America: The Study of the Indian and the Idea of Civilization* (Baltimore, 1965); and John T. Flanagan, who edited *William Joseph Snelling's Tales of the Northwest* (Minneapolis, 1936). Text references are to Flanagan's edition. An earlier version of my remarks on Snelling's book appeared in "The Half-Breed in Snelling's *Tales of the Northwest*," *The Old Northwest* 2 (1976): 141–51. Permission to use this material has been generously granted by Miami University, Ohio.

39. Pearce, *Savages of America*, pp. 220–22.

40. Interestingly, Snelling's complaints about judicial policy and procedure are standard in recent Indian studies; see Francis Paul Prucha, *American Indian Policy in the Formative Years* (Cambridge, Mass., 1962), pp. 195–98.

41. Robert Edson Lee, *From West to East: Studies in the Literature of the American West* (Urbana, Ill., 1966), p. 57.

42. See Herbert Ross Brown, *The Sentimental Novel in America, 1789–1860* (Durham, N.C., 1940), p. 170.

43. Ibid., p. 171.

44. Ibid., p. 364.

45. L. Augustus Jones, *Bloody Brook; or the Bride of Plymouth Rock* (New York, 1866), p. 93. Text references are to this edition.

46. Nathaniel Hawthorne, *Septimius Felton*, in *The Elixir of Life Manuscripts* (Columbus, Ohio, 1977), pp. 84, 148. Text references are to this edition. The character of Felton seems to have been strongly influenced by Hawthorne's impression of Thoreau, to whom he referred as apparently "inclined to lead a sort of Indian life among civilized men" (*The American Notebooks*, ed. Claude M. Simpson [Columbus, Ohio, 1972], p. 354). See also Chapter 4, note 1, below.

47. *The Piazza Tales*, vol. 10 in *The Works of Herman Melville* (London, 1923), p. 236. Certain misreadings of Hunilla evident in I. Newberry's "The Encantadas: Melville's *Inferno*" (*American Literature* 38 [1966]: 49–68) are redressed in David A. Roberts's reading of her purgatorial endurance as no genuine resolution of the problems of existence ("Structure and Meaning in Melville's 'The Encantadas,'" *ESQ: A Journal of the American Renaissance* 22 [1976]:235–44). Cf. Peruvian Cabaco in *Moby-Dick*.

48. *Piazza Tales*, pp. 233, 235. In an apparent newspaper source for Melville's story, Hunilla is not a half-blood: see Robert Sattelmeyer and James Barbour, "The Sources and Genesis of Melville's 'Norfolk Isle and the Chola Widow,'" *American Literature* 50 (1978):398–417.

49. See Alexander Cowie, *The Rise of the American Novel* (New York, 1951), p. 173; and Benjamin Lease, *That Wild Fellow John Neal and the American Literary Revolution* (Chicago, 1972), p. 144. A much more ex-

tensive version of my remarks on Neal's novel appeared in "Power, Authority, and Revolutionary Impulse in John Neal's *Rachel Dyer*," *Studies in American Fiction* 4 (1976):143–55.

50. John Neal, *Rachel Dyer: A North American Story* (Portland, Maine, 1828), pp. 21, 249. Page references for subsequent quotations from this edition are included parenthetically in the text. A half-blood also appears in Neal's enigmatic and badly neglected *Logan: A Family History* (Philadelphia, 1822).

51. The word power is not only prevalent in *Rachel Dyer* but abounds in Neal's writings. It is power that Neal admires in Cooper's *The Refugee* and that he perceives as his own strongest attribute; see Neal's *American Writers: A Series of Papers Contributed to "Blackwood's Magazine"* (1824–1825), ed. Fred Lewis Pattee (Durham, N.C., 1937), pp. 220–21; 244–46.

52. Despite his sources, Neal makes free with historical details, even quite clearly telling us he does so in his addendum to the novel. A detailed discussion of this point appears in my essay on Neal (see note 49), and all that need be repeated here are the facts that Mary Dyer gave birth to no daughers, and that no Quakers were placed on trial during the Salem disturbance. Neal was raised a Quaker but broke with the faith; nevertheless, his personal feelings apparently did not interfere with his use of Quakerism to symbolize certain features of his notion of a proper American. In the late seventeenth century and the early eighteenth century, European literature apparently identified the Quakers with the Indians; the identification occurs, as well, in nineteenth-century American works: see Slotkin, *Regeneration through Violence*, pp. 203–05, 510–12.

53. Michael Colacurcio, "Footsteps of Ann Hutchinson: The Context of *The Scarlet Letter*," *English Literary History*, 39 (1972):473. Neal's suggestion that Ann Hutchinson is a type for Rachel may have been seminal to Hawthorne's interest in her as a type for Hester; and Rachel's symbolic residence between the colonists and the Indians as well as the symbolic cap confining her hair, among other matters, adumbrate similar details in *The Scarlet Letter*. Nina Baym's "Passion and Authority in *The Scarlet Letter*" (*New England Quarterly* 43 [1970]:209–30), read in the light of my discussion, suggests still other similarities between the two novels. Lease refers to Hawthorne's addiction to Neal's romances (*That Wild Fellow*, pp. 39, 94–95, 194), and possibly memory of *Rachel Dyer* influenced Hawthorne's decision to make the protagonist of *Septimius Felton* a mixed-blood Indian.

54. In fact the real Mary Dyer, who had no daughters, was a close friend of Ann Hutchinson and was executed in 1660 for her Quaker heresy. Neal's references to Hutchinson, so central to his view of Rachel, advance his favorable position on women's rights. For his views on this subject,

see Neal, *Wandering Recollections of a Somewhat Busy Life* (Boston, 1869), pp. 50–51, 88–103, 412–20; and Boyd Guest, "John Neal and 'Women's Rights and Women's Wrongs,'" *New England Quarterly* 18 (1945):505–15.

55. Neal married in the same year *Rachel Dyer* was published. In his autobiography he speaks of his horror of "the dreariness, the loneliness, the desolation, the utter hopelessness of a bachelor's life," indicating the value of marriage as a symbol for him at the time (*Wandering Recollections*, p. 356). Hawthorne also emphasized this symbolic meaning of marriage in *The Scarlet Letter*.

56. Joseph Fletcher uses this phrase to describe an approach to morality which is not limited by rigid notions based on natural law (Roman Catholicism) or on scriptural law (Protestantism) and which prevents the other extreme of antinomianism by admitting the single absolute of love as the criterion for a moral decision (*Situation Ethics: The New Morality* [Philadelphia, 1966]).

57. Neal, *American Writers*, p. 201.

58. On Neal's use of the colloquial, see Harold C. Martin, "The Colloquial Tradition in the Novel," *New England Quarterly* 32 (1959):459; and his "The Development of Style in 19th Century American Fiction," in *Style in Prose Fiction*, ed. H. C. Martin (New York, 1959), pp. 114–41.

CHAPTER FOUR

1. Of tangential interest, Leslie Fiedler has defined the western story as "a fiction dealing with the confrontation in the wilderness of a transplanted WASP and a radically alien other, an Indian—leading either to a metamorphosis of the WASP into something neither White nor Red (sometimes by adoption, sometimes by sheer emulation, but *never* by actual miscegenation), or else to the annihilation of the Indian" (*The Return of the Vanishing American* [New York, 1968], p. 24). The Henry David Thoreau of *A Week on the Concord and Merrimack Rivers* (1849) and of "the connecting link between wild and cultivated fields" in *Walden* (1854) self-consciously adopted the status of a half-blood in spirit.

2. *The Works of James Fenimore Cooper* (New York, 1895–1900), 5: 125. Text references are to this edition. Apparently during Cooper's lifetime "only roving bands of degenerate half-breed Indians frequented" the Lake Otsego region of New York with which Cooper was familiar (Albert Keiser, *The Indian in American Literature* [New York, 1933], pp. 101–02).

3. Most evidently Leslie Fiedler, in *Love and Death in the American Novel* (Cleveland, 1962), pp. 202–10. See George Dekker's reply in *James Fenimore Cooper the Novelist* (London, 1967), pp. 64–83. On the other hand, Edwin Fussell's claim that Cooper surreptitiously advocates mis-

cegenation seems dubious (*Frontier: American Literature and the American West* [Princeton, N.J., 1965], p. 42).

4. Michael D. Butler, "Narrative Structure and Historical Process in *The Last of the Mohicans,*" *American Literature* 48 (1976):136.

5. Richard Slotkin, *Regeneration through Violence: The Mythology of the American Frontier, 1600–1860* (Middletown, Conn., 1973), pp. 394–465. Nicholas J. Karolides provides a study of the Boone figure in the literature of the twentieth century in *The Pioneer in the American Novel, 1900–1950* (Norman, Okla., 1967).

6. Ann S. Stephens, *Malaeska: The Indian Wife of the White Hunter* (New York, 1929), p. 33. Text references are to this edition. Other works by Stephens that include half-bloods are: *Mary Derwent* (*Ladies Companion*, 1838; Philadelphia, 1858); *Ahmo's Plot; or the Governor's Indian Child* (New York, 1863); and *Mahaska: The Indian Princess* (New York, 1863).

7. Albert W. Aiken, *The Indian Mazeppa; or, The Madman of the Plains. A Strange Story of the Texas Frontier* (New York, 1878), p. 45.

8. In securing her release from some bandits, Isabel Escobedo successfully buys the aid of Jose, a half-blood cook who is not presented as utterly evil. As Isabel explains to her sister, "Half-breeds are notoriously treacherous and cunning. I know the race for I have been used to them since I was a child. Their greed, too, is great and there is a far better chance that we will be able to bribe him than if he was a full-blooded Mexican, or in fact a man of any other nation" (*The Fresh on the Rio Grande; or, the Red Riders of Rayon. A Story of the Texan Frontier* [New York, 1887], p. 15). Easily bought loyalty also characterizes Lupe Escato, a half-blood hired killer who is known as The Snake and who is "about as ugly a customer as can be scared up in Arizona" (Albert W. Aiken, *Dick Talbot, the Ranch King; or, the Double Foe. A Romance of the Hawks of Cababi* [New York, 1892], p. 5; cf. pp. 17–18).

9. Albert W. Aiken, *Talbot in Apache Land; or, Dick Buckskin, the Man of Mettle* (New York, 1892), p. 11. Text references are to this edition.

10. *The Writings of Bret Harte* (Boston, 1896–1914), 11:252. Text references are to this edition. For the dates of the first appearance of Harte's stories, I have relied on Joseph Gaer's *Bret Harte: Bibliography and Biographical Data* (New York, 1968). For a good enumeration of pertinent works by Harte, see Margaret Duckett, "Bret Harte's Portrayal of Half-Breeds," *American Literature* 25 (1953:193–212).

11. George R. Stewart, Jr., mentions Harte's Jewish grandfather and suggests that his sympathetic portraits of mixed-blood individuals derived from his sensitivity to the matter (*Bret Harte: Argonaut and Exile* [Boston, 1931], p. 16).

12. In *Old Hicks, the Guide* (New York, 1848) Charles Webber reports an Indian initiation ceremony in which white men are dyed red as a sign of their new membership in the tribe.

13. In *Buffalo Bill and the Ke-Week Totem; or, Pawnee Bill's Blacksnake Magic* (New York, 1917), by an anonymous writer, a thief and murderer named Tex Rankin stains himself so that he looks like a half-blood—half Indian, half Mexican. But the removal of this stain at the end of the story does not signal Rankin's redemption; the half-blood persona, with "beady eyes" and "ill-omened grin," simply objectifies the maliciousness of the person it seems to disguise.

14. Duckett, "Bret Harte's Portrayal of Half-Breeds," p. 199.

CHAPTER FIVE

1. Roy Harvey Pearce, *The Savages of America: The Study of the Indian and the Idea of Civilization* (Baltimore, 1965), p. 194.

2. In *The Negro in American Fiction* (Washington, D.C., 1937), Sterling Brown indicates that the mulatto is presented in fiction as more rebellious, militant, and aspiring than full-blooded blacks, and as unhappy and tragic because of the conflict between his desire to be white and the necessity of aligning himself with the black race. Unavailable for review at the time my manuscript was being typeset was Judith R. Berzon's *Neither Black Nor White: The Mulatto Character in American Fiction* (New York, 1978).

3. Caroline Kirkland, *Western Clearings* (London, 1846), p. 211. Apparently this attitude was rare; see William G. McLaughlin, "Red Indians, Black Slavery and White Racism: America's Slaveholding Indians," *American Quarterly* 26 (1974): 367–85.

4. William Gilmore Simms, *The Wigwam and the Cabin* (New York, 1856), p. 374. Text references are to this edition.

5. This strategy may have been reinforced by the fact that some Indians, particularly in New England, esteemed black over white skin as a color of beauty (James Axtell, "The Ethnology of Early America: A Review Essay," *William and Mary Quarterly* 35 [1978]:67).

6. See Chadwick Hansen, "The Metamorphosis of Tituba," *New England Quarterly* 47 (1974):3–12.

7. Victor W. Turner, *The Forest of Symbols: Aspects of Ndembu Ritual* (Ithaca, N.Y., 1967); and idem, *The Ritual Process: Structure and Anti-Structure* (Chicago, 1969).

8. See especially the first chapter of Erving Goffman's *Stigma* (Englewood Cliffs, N.J., 1969).

9. Mary Douglas, *Purity and Danger: An Analysis of Concepts of Pollution and Taboo* (London, 1966).

Index ∾